© https://www.beneinst.it

Gerardo D'Orrico was born in Cosenza on March 6, 1976. After completing my high school I attended the universities of Arcavacata (CS) and Bologna but without a degree, I have a good knowledge of computer science and some musical instruments. My youth was between the residence of Luzzi (CS) and Cosenza for studies or in the hometown of my mother Villapiana (CS) by the sea. I have made many trips in Italy and someone abroad, after the military service I helped my father with his work and I dedicated myself to writing prose as well as continuing my passion for computer science and software programming, I created and manage a web-site (beneinst.it) where everyone can enter their pages for free: letters, poems, drawings, pictures, photos. So far I have published four books: 1. The good and the bad, memories 2. An ash ceiling 3. We Are Already Ten Minutes Ago 4. Say it yourself. I live in Luzzi where, among other occupations, I continue to write or revise my texts and research for technological art.

Youth photo

Gerardo D'Orrico

It`s Already Us In Ten Minutes

Diary

Preface

This diary is the third book written by me, an exploration of urban and suburban environments to observe humans and modern objects. Representations in philosophical or mathematical form in order to find the right amount of motion, proof that good is a higher feeling certainly than evil, the right repetition of always the same things to confirm that here you can not say the false is much less realize it. A certain practicality that can be associated with a manual on socio-political rights, then the different forms of exit from a modern unhealthy or incorporeal being. The becoming of one's own experiences, of one's own dreams in their reality, without basic problems to confirm an overall human evidence, finally the transfer of social and anthropic material so much contested in these years after the year two thousand. The period of the twenty-one letters contained reaches from December 2008 to July 2010, english translation by Fatima Immacolata Pretta. Good reading,

Gerardo D'Orrico

1.
Your dark rooms

31.12.2008

"Hello you had to start somewhere, you could start by removing what you are not, what they make you understand for yourself or belong to you more... your deep teasing."

The attempt to make people understand verb or action, who or the other study that openly leads us to the most disturbing delinquent, the divine possibility of not believing or not being. One day of celebration is also the next, the reality is always that, we moved to feel that true, you are in evil? ...and yet it's so difficult, still for a while eh, you usually repeat a case, you have to accept it or better you have to build a law, a solution on daily horrors in forms, acts forced in that way. Those damn troubles make our life a sweetness, there we see well forward but no one has ever spoken of thieves here, who is the first to say what we live today and who exists. Thousands of rules to respect, rules without ever saying that that error is not part of life, your commitment to others is your presence even in your absence. Errors, commissions, naval ports, land areas view or accuracy, you think that it is a false life or fallacious, what it says here will go in a software package or something else.

What I don't know, they explain in two lines just to keep quiet, they don't have to make fun of us are people those things, different individuals create the difference in your vacuum, everything there is exists from zero on. Here the ruler is evil! I almost suffocate again... they'll denounce us ah, and then they've never done anything, they won't get anything out of it. We live addicted and bored that afterwards it's like before, it's not just on this particular occasion, what you wanted to tell me later we'll talk about it. They seem to me a shadow on the world no necessity, just the total absence of everything, where and when to go, leave to leave an unhealthy. All things forbidden that are good but, the truth remains a road without mistakes, after all there is no other bad, they want to take us to a part where we do not exist, where there is no me as an idea or, as a person for example, an open field where there is no one, then there kill us forever. One key is that you are here, no one left because you were missing, while the false as the cold shower, are five hundred books to read to know.

Here an exchange of person is normal, being here is just an expletive, it will be the air we breathe nobody does anything, it seems the usual song is instead life, what sadness what has been created by the indifference of the tragedy. Whoever wins is cancelled by mistake and that's it, it's all wrong to get out of here you need to call the law, the police or a lawyer beause it's not a dream or the other, but a tragedy of others in your life. People complain that 'the future is the past, the existence of another is necessary to distinguish the parties, a hundred points for all people that is not dead. There is always an explanation why we are alive, what we do, are doing it as the opposite but then only one act has arisen the lytics of these times that modern times are passed but smell of centuries ago, as true as the blindness that we bring, more true still, more true, here is a unique reality, all 'the world has changed, people and measures is not true, it is not past but present the future. Words that have a taste of constant renewal, like a rebirth under a new sign. Renewal is renewal, anti-death in life. Dangerous business they say, better would be others steal, thieves of beautiful things that have always been and will be the right ones, while others know nothing of the impossible things. The immobility of a movement creates an inner resurgence, no one will denounce us is just too much fear of that thing that no one has solved, changed. The music is over now where you go alone, there are things that shine, others of gold.

After lunch I'll have to leave again, I'll go where this place doesn't exist anymore, the memory is the access key, if you want to lose a key to enter the house, we have almost nothing left. You still have some of those orange blossoms in this war without borders, since yesterday it still persists today, it does not want to end up continuous as life is recurring or, continue for a fake that to call it already feels better, and we are still here, me or you, the many of those who will be fantasy.

Solutions in this world are endless or, better to say under a million, in this period that the world has changed it is said that it is over, but finally it is just another while it is already day, the light will come again, there are only many more of us as many things have not been done also this year, the folds of the past, it seems to take a degree to understand your time, to complain or judge there is always space but, what you wanted where it is, what really exists. My dream is life, will there be joy where a state is installed, where these problems no longer exist?! The present will no longer be past, like the mud on rhetoric, it is what we will have ten minutes before, half an hour before or the day before now.

A harmony of voices is words that conquer us, an extraordinary interest at breakfast, a strange world to say the least envelops us to continue the day, stuffed is embellished with an unknown identity that everyone chooses, if bad or ugly for me, is the worst possible situation today instead. Those who must speak must be helped, those who say that that speech is wrong, those who free is for a few, in the sarcasm of tragedy, who speaks is the solution. Base not obvious but completion of another work, which must be finished, not fraudulent of a disappearance in life or, illegal and legal. Enlightened, I stay home with a few friends and family. Photocopies of life or words in other situations, you know what has already passed sometimes does not return, it is certain that someone is offended, perhaps insulting is not good so it has always been better alone, in parallel universes, all earthly, simple and cheated. Allowing the reality of a wrong knowledge, unhealthy and its quantity, does not create concrete things to be clear, if they were not impostors even in the past, remember those negative things then, today you will see what a complication if the problem is inserted again, it seems like we were born yesterday where we live. Remaining in the past is another thing, by the way, it will also be the business of our company today where we are, like the mathematical thought of what we wanted to present the future, instead it was a remote past but, not a verb like time... ok thanks, continuing you will find your exes and stories where you cannot lie.

The day that has no taste, colourless people who interest us, where we will have made a mistake, we are not here or in these parts, already let's leave that thing alone then, it was not too far ahead will be just words and, obscene matters of blood. Invented also 'the fact that no one solves, you go up from the ground floor to the eightieth only with an elevator that was built then, placed in that place for that reason. Look outside the house, you don't have to make fun of me if the reality has to be explained is people, in short I am what you say. Do what you want to do if it's right or okay for you, you know how many objects even thoughts were forbidden long ago, respecting the law everything is allowed, it was not true that here is wrong or everything is forbidden, to think about it well is ignorance or power. The master does evil there.

What? Boxes, hidden objects that have no light of experience from ignorance, from forgetfulness, after all it was the same this piece of furniture, is what it is about, it is said what is concrete. Don't ever stop already, then the batteries run out, so what does it matter somewhere you had to finish but, it's absence of state, absence of those wonderful laws that would make us more beautiful that instead make us continue roughly so: me, you then all are always more or the opposite stop, it was forbidden even this solid years ago, say or do without fault of who it was, as we are true contemporaries.

A wrong blood group, with the wrong story and then silences, nothing worse but someone is informed about the future that is no longer a bad thing, okay but it is also beyond already, it has always been known, someone says it because he has taken the wrong road but, for this reason too, there is a path. We travel together with the world, and we are already absurd things in the wrong places, even just to make us make mistakes could seem the state instead it was evil, and I told you everything. Now the things to be said have multiplied, they're getting faster while a basic procedure has already been called for a good or, therefore, for a human encounter that has already been modified before. It's all by chance, Madam, or, it's a bad thing to throw away, who hasn't made us sew our complete dress. A software is not recommended to me by a friend, the State or other, but a study of personal sectors, understood as a future to avoid.

It ends where you've gone, in the speeches you make, a very slight question sometimes just software but present as the mistakes you do not make, things no one will see, the people you frequent. What you did, what you expect, what deleted you in the program, what you had to do that you didn't realize. The concept exists, you can't delete it, they want to make you forget it as superfluous, maybe you think they will make you forget what you have to do, but, you only forget the act you had to do, and it's already a crime it belongs to the creator, you will remember where the boat will land, the bank. After all, that's the way things went, nobody said anything and everything disappeared.

Look around you go over the fiery hill, you are reborn becoming yourself again after a mistake, on this planet at the end of the year zero eight, of infinite forms, some people push saying in a while you finish, nothing will happen again, instead you continue, so now this is life. You are a good thing, your duty is a single thing, you have to do what was good once upon a time, what you didn't do remains for later, like your dark rooms. Where there is no one, you should spend the whole day, the whole life.

Other, other speeches afterwards will all be wrong, it seems like the wind is blowing against us. What you did not accept will come back, like what was said sinning not to be true, even if only to do the same things and then to die, nobody tells us how things are, you just talk, you can't do anything for those badly built realities, who are those then, who is after all your great person, an incorrect Italian after a catastrophe of millions of people, in silence.

The problem is at the beginning, once explained its fundamental entities for this existence, it gets better and better, as sometimes words consume themselves, without even being said. If you want everything for us, if you find the cornerstones for which the decisions are, steal it but what, the day is already over, beyond everything and all the things to love and say, there is to make order in the chaos of our injustices, after all that has not been done in this past year, it will never end, instead you look better or you turn around and it's walready over, as other objectivities have become three-dimensional objects, that's how important they are.

Too much is too much, you only succeed on one side where it was right to go before, after all the most effective. Flowers that 'the day ends behind its light, inside an evening that does not end if not in Rome ends. At the end of the end, after only we leave anyway, so as not to return to the place where we weren't there at that hour, where life begins to create itself in history. We are all that life needs, if we are the ones who change nothing abnormal happens, it is already solved what they are looking for, panting for people you see passing under the window of the house. Sometimes you just have to talk, sometimes it's just a little too spicy, like in a city that you can't do anything, because we don't already exist, try talking to that strange guy of our friend to see what he thinks about the situation.

Tell him, how can I tell you, that you're not in it anymore. I'm still sleepy breathing, advice here is expensive.

Bye G.

2.
Elderly age

31.01.2009

To live or to remain without the possibility of not believing in the good, and to know when you have been robbed. I imagine so also my third age or, a journey into loneliness, such a confrontation that life cannot betray, much worse than to say a marriage. Certainly a political relationship interested in a social part of us when we were young, the imaginative view of the present with its never-ending developments, a moment in life made not only of memories but, of a deep knowledge and whole consciousness.

A mirror to know is that dark evil that takes away the light from the true truth, that still escapes the word, the actions or the works that we all dream of being present. I know that place where you want us to meet again, where you said it was better to see each other or, how many steps there are for that beyond that knows a lot of this way, how terrestrial is that monster that you need to avoid, and it is still there that does not know what you want, every problem arises where the competence to argue ends. The fundamental axis of displacement towards the third age is not a problem, given the large number of people and ideas that carry us forward the day, it would be better to erase the loneliness. The universal starts from the world that has changed, words are even more useful than before, like a capacious object in our city, it seems to be all at stake as when we were children, we do not know what happened not for the real but, it goes for the dream that is said to be interrupted because it is in the air, not in the aqueducts of our Main City that nobody can say, which for everyone is so. Sometimes it is difficult to speak, often we are prevented by those temporal causes, where we do not correspond with reality we dissociate ourselves from the present or rather from the recent past.

While the century is going, we remain as others say we do, and then it goes on, or it worked the future prospects are really varied, not a canon of ideas that that party wants you to believe. Belief is dear in these times, even if an erasure cannot last forever, the century of good is already recovering, a light in the picture at sunset or, at dawn, heals wounds. Our address, our memories, the dream sometimes appears, one is no longer alone which is better. Afterwards you will see the taste inside, a nothing to the taste of gunpowder, so they still tell us that it is not us or, that this speech goes out of the line, a world of rubbish but certainly not wrong to speak our concrete thought.

Loneliness a subject like other unsocial, like being death or empty space, sometimes it's the words that don't come out of your mouth or you can't get them out yourself, it's everyday problems not to talk about it. A tangle of absences and essences that do not build, weights of temporal measures, of what you will do next, of space and above all old age, what it will be to be old. All in one place, in a mine, the false, the profane, the things that are not good, the real current living situation, the real name of what you are looking for, the taste of sweet and bad then, you will tell me not me to you what you have to say or do, a sort of thing that resembles the heart, study or read about the time that passes between a pause and the other then happened, you add what is yours.

Old age must never lead to loneliness because, the present can be future, here words sometimes escape, as I have heard many wrong ideas, for example we are already dead or others say that we are not whole, complete or completed, we will be old we want absolute peace. The problem it was that nobody knows what is proposed is nothing, how serious it was the possibility of saying one thing at a time or, if something cannot be you.

That strange wave from where it came from, it never happened to you, be careful who you talk to, nobody says they know anything while the abuse and injustice are passed by law, they tell you to go on living, as written history is reality, the truth then betray themselves. At night at three or four in the morning you can see better what happened the day before, how can you say I don't know, remember it's not a personal task what you are looking at. Someone lives in the wrong place, we are the wrong ones, we are all going to end up the same way as nothing, better to say it's not all at will, we have never said who is bad or who has won, it seems but it takes strength to rise again, that's how much in the year zero nine, see there are those who think that 'the good is past and the future as before, it's a matter of regularity or, of percentage increases in itself, people come later, life is after death, it's a legal matter what you don't say, people are beyond everything, it's real not a fake.

A day like any other the discovery of America, strange as many things on this planet are strange, with the cadences of a universe in between, issues so big that the several thousand people involved made confusion. Waning Moon seems like a movie I've already seen, stop the lobotomy, remember who said it must end dear minister representative of the State or, where was it completed? seemed like small problems instead are memory lapses, disagreements or discords between our loved ones then, we are constantly beaten otherwise we saw better, pause. America who knows what you're doing today, it's better to continue on the ground too many films that are being discussed. Being old is not as wrong as being young but, just a great repentance, then you need a division of the parties, so for horror to say blame.

It's better to rest and wait, where we live it's not quiet, there's no appetite anymore, words are not just words sometimes saying them is already an abuse, just thinking is not right. Wars, persistence and beliefs that approach the walls of what? Sometimes if you don't speak, you don't understand what's wrong with what they've done to you, according to the government you'll do everything by yourself, have fun you'll become a thing not a construction, you can't find the accounts without punches, we'll continue but the air is so sharp almost suffocating. We want the will and power while no one will solve those problems, we are already well, the good pay is convincing us but, it exists now, today in how many cuts we have, how low they have sent us, on the other hand no one insults only the air, for example if you keep your head still on one side you see that it is solved, while on the other without you noticing, the same thing is not solved. Sing today: good has been obliterated, he who recovers has been lynched for sorcerer or witch, fantasy governs.

The dream is where you were, where you can't imagine it. Where were you five minutes ago who had arrived? It's very difficult to have a whole person show up here, it's very rare what you had to go and do, many times it wasn't even your job, just take a look at your personal defence, just run away. The dream, the nightmare doesn't want to end, the relationship has become absurd, understand me if one wants to continue alone, we are not awake yet. The idiocy is great when you put, by the way, life can become a waste of time, like believing that what comes from the East is good! Soon the boys are already eighteen years old, it's if you watch on video the solution to all our problems exists, you know that the air of lies is not here, but around here.

They say that including the complaint goes all to one side, like a train that passes over the road you are traveling, instead nothing is not coming, nothing will be done, they are the culprits, old age, the dream that does not want to end or maybe something under the teeth. Stunned remained the world when they declared the truth, existences said as they are and, we are still here, did you know the beyond the grave? with a little 'calm you clarify a screen full of blood.

After the Sabbath comes a quiet day, peace is for everyone but, strange if you look around there is not even the air of what was supposed to be, there are people who ask me about the structure of good, what you want as soon as you get up you cannot do evil, I'm awake for about fifteen minutes strange life, does not disappear is assimilated, overcome. As long as that climb or a staircase of more than a thousand steps, so tell me is not gone, the other one is gone, you've already heard the words of this last part of my speech: it's not guilt but, belief in God.

In the secret of the words, lies your main interest. As the world stalls watching, people, colours.

Our traps are the big words that deal with small people during this disaster. The incredulity of people is like the force that is not expressed to realize our energy, our conquest, that does not know it is not us.

It was reality our dream but better not discuss the emptiness, because we are all the same, is still the place the other day was called Equilibrium as 'l film, that is a swastika without extended arms from the sides, while that goes, do not look at it. Anyway we'll become old, we'll listen, we'll watch, we'll lose everything to make a long story short then, check what you find and go back to your room at home without instructions, you'll see you don't understand well you think but, actually you're fine. Talking yes to grow up but, it's a great work of words from emptiness to disownment, of the individual person, just look at the rain that falls while those who still want to lure us, still alive also dresses as an old man or a couple, a single but it's always him or her, it's called and is the horrendous.

So we are one step away from paradise is for no reason you can have everything ahead, a complaint seems a must, where you go I do not walk in another room, you will see there are no solutions to a problem already solved that someone says, if not his only solution. Whoever thinks that once the problem is solved, that is, you or I will be left with nothing, in the memory of what was or who was there, goes too fast... this was a help. Lobotomy, demagnetization of consciousness and memory, past or recent. I think you live but everything else is as boring as the song, you live yes but down, the reasons for not being a great person, the superior advantage, freedom is the same for everyone if you understand what is a word of blasphemy then, the speech continues. The hour is delayed I think I'll finish writing for a while, it's really difficult to talk with a contemporary especially today that will be January. If we are always in a room where those things are, I wanted to tell you a few years ago, if you don't come out of it, mistakes are always more and more but, if you think about it, the thought is nothing if you look in front of who you are talking to, they are not mistakes of our company but of the air.

I know the balance is important but if you want a translator for every common feeling, word or situation, we haven't understood the good yet. When everything is lost, nothing is lost, people lack the word as misfortune is part of our life. Do you want to keep drinking? There is no such thing as emptiness, not me but the air has changed, you don't understand it's no longer here or, you're not here, therefore was evil. Life is after more other things that they don't say on television, like that we have to be helped like an old man, as if life goes on without what I don't know, then you do it if you don't ask for your imposed key It. There's no one here. Oh, come on, the world's already over, I'm kidding.

Bye, G.

3.
The dynamics of the pancreas

28.02.2009

Prison has already been left where the heart wasn't there, is it your spot that leads you to betray yourself or what? It's the classic that leads us. It was who, his last robbery or usurpation, we have already been numbered with a bar code, articles or codes in words that last at least a whole day. Only with a plan you will never be able to get out of this habitat, Italy pulsates badly now we are all correct anarchists, whoever moves is already dead or stabbed.

When they go away our memories already end up there in their super powers, where their joint-stock company, the spa, begins. The horrendous is clear in too many things, too many confusions, the humans, the integers want to know when they were inaugurated? Never, it's yet to begin. After the meal you start to feel better, bitter or sour. You're a quality bitter, branded, you're a past tense, you know that everyone here knows each other very well.

Confusion is always part of that thing that makes us study, we jump from the dead to the past future. In the afternoon silence is everything, nobody has understood the evil, don't leave him in the deception of being you, it's a strong trap to your experience, where you don't say you are.

Line up, alienate yourself, your law is formality. Quintals of suppressed ideas, those monsters are obscene creatures, whoever acts in one direction cannot do something parallel to the opposite, whoever will not be defeated, evil is defeated the very moment you write it. Who knows it didn't happen, maybe we are the evidence, the humans of the indicated production, why don't you talk to your neighbour today, never been to Canada, too many taboos see only narrow words, then an evil sun rises, you don't understand what good is. You think it's there instead is where no one says it is, how all this will be erased, the power of those who exist or who have done it is no longer spoken of. Years could still pass and everyone will still live for evil, then excuse me for not talking, you can't get up from this infinite vortex, certainly it's the day yesterday betrayed you, as you see there is only the road, where and when. It is certainly a story of others but where you are, you must not believe in death in life, it is a story of children who become never grown up and have to be treated in a prison, it is a tragedy of other loved ones that happens today at home or, another drama where no one will stay then, otherwise we will be in one place, so you wanted the youth to call where people are and you know everyone, otherwise they will be laws of belonging to other people is away so for the whole day. Living evil don't you say what you think? Go back to where? then that wasn't the way, you don't even say that humans are lost because you don't need to do evil. Who has closed us, there is no way, don't you look that it's not your private problem, people are lost for theirs, as individuals meet while the next ones move away.

It's amazing not to smoke too much, I hate those good ideas that make the present thought pass for a state of passage. I've seen that there are so many him, so many her, not just one character plus the evils of our city, so many for every place or house, that's how we avoid them. What will have happened to the downstairs or fasting, the point then that you just have to breathe, feel how expensive the air is. What was true somewhere will be true, breathe in phases, smoke or, have you got the beam? In quiet, an attack on politics at twenty at night which is worse than... but you don't understand that the emptiness. Theme: the serious waste of time, ten more years. Look at him all his life your vulgar, disintegrated to go where, after they decided not to speak anymore. What happens is boredom, what should be today without problems, look how many people are already in a crime against people. Roman boredom, today and tomorrow what do you think you live in Calabria.

Our software to live is wrong or, has been hacked more even who tells you, the separation of assets should be called this thing that goes around the city, not dear citizen. The taste of good things is true, the taste of bad things, the things you can know are the things you are able to understand and it's already all wrong, the bad of already as well as death is part of your life. An act of denunciation surpasses everything you know, you live well or in the good, even if only because the evening has come, like the surprise with the trouble that life told you, so begins the discourse of what you have lived, what you have not done because you have been. You've seen how many people come into us and say this is where the party is, they are strong and winning. You've been denounced and yet everyone wants to do as you or I do, tomorrow it will all be illegal. Who wants to talk if they arrest him right after he opens his mouth, it'll be other people's problem. Are our word or mouth dirty? You want peace, you have to call yourself. Soon it won't last ten minutes then jail, where did you get lost because you're too compromised? OK.

Most problems are the same for everyone, then better to go and finish the evening in the kitchen. Ok, the speech is long, from the confusion you risk to do nothing, too many things not said but you know, not done. The solution is beyond evil, a declaration of not belonging to them, then you find yourself, true. That noise you hear wants to enter your house, as in every house in our city, is evil, you can't talk while there you see them passing fast under your house. Remissive every time, still those problems that the usual people are hunting, is what you have never told yourself, someone runs away from their reality. The concrete of people is universally opposed to our idea of the day, the world will cease to exist you have some idea about it.

Unspeakable problems with wordless explanations, the solution is to go without stopping, nonexistent problems of theirs without the head, pure obstacles. The law always governs because even after you see the light of day, the question that has asked you is not yours, you will see tomorrow. It's a national questionnaire, there's no one in the room. Their friends don't overcome evil, they are evil. Let's change the subject with then mambo, we are already finished and we have to pay, I know you don't have to talk but, you can laugh at our experience that nobody says real, you look somewhere else then you will see where or what you will think tomorrow, where someone believes.

The helplessness of ignorance, of what you do not want, experiences or horrible things where we live in Calabria, you thought there was a letter, black on a white sheet of paper, instead there was nothing, but there is hell and death, more than the flesh is the organs that you have on you then, nothing more than nothing, alone! Continuing the evening that ends, you will see the light of a new day, better the law and ... in short it is nothing tomorrow, it will be one day less on Earth, the rest of a day's work. It seems to me it's time for this umpteenth murder to sleep, what is a criminal offense.

Bipolar, tonight I have nothing to do, I am writing to tell you about this evening so far away that words are lost, there are no more reasons to live here, where you say you are present in the world, you do not live by what you say, who exceeds has the keys, so where you stay is where to be alive or dead, memories and past things, the disgust or gratitude of what was to tell you have done us evil, maybe you know where you think you live, then see what you did wrong or how you do not return. The others are not there to recognize those problems that you can't find or, you don't search, you say where you got lost. We are great now, our time is much past in the future. It will be a night where those who want do not, rest is none of our business, if you do not act against yourself or do evil, what can normalcy.

You know it's nice to live here so dear, maybe you know me I don't tell you anything anymore, since you are not here, those look like scissors but, you didn't lose, you didn't get lost, there should be a doctor for the rest, we weren't even supposed to have a society where we had to do everything ourselves, where you don't talk so as not to make mistakes or, if you lose you lost forever, so be careful. Memories, stop if you want to understand what is happening there you have to avoid, even what people who have not thought are saying.

The code of words are the facts that do not change, it has been working for years but it is always better to rest, to avoid, not to do in short. Contact is a loss: Saturday night what did you do, during the week or if you got married. What you know you do not support, not the unresolved while everything has a name, all the things described but someone talks about it, it is a very heavy reality your life for public duties. Today it's like that, tomorrow who knows, you still believe that I don't see, look it's not the same as them what they lost. Incongruous situations where you are not there, you will grow up and you will understand until the end, in which century you live is certainly that dark shadow above and around you that pretends not to achieve, to get inside you then tonight, you know on this side the evening is very special, full of humans the day they have not done anything, for the usual and serious issues. Whose fault is it? We are a bit shabby to say this, each of us knows whose fault it is as many other things are colored. The blame is of what was said long ago, I think, what happened to say to be recognizable is already for a long time the same, not for five minutes or ten minutes., it is the transparency of our body another thing, we repair ourselves not to lose blood all 'the rest of the day ... and it was already everything as the leaves fly in winter, the streets and streets with the good taste of what it was, the work must be done. Alone in our small group, you can deal with matters that know the state that the eyes gratify, always the usual confusion in the past days, now they are sure to talk about something else and that the others do not talk about them because it is too much, so leeches are things that are not said by mistakes or, by simplicity, so we have lost that we cannot be called except in front of a lawyer, from how they have arranged us, it would be better to turn on the television. I'm going to see if there's any coffee left in the kitchen, in the summary of a week where the world won't stay, what you want to know won't stay inside us. The first instinct, the rest of the Earth that revolves around us, without or with us, vitamins or medicines, after all, if you look where there isn't any, don't swallow them.

What to do or what air, senses, impulse, expres sion will give us. It's better not to be controversial about the weather, today and yesterday's thunderstorms are already made of what will happen.

Bye, G.

4.
Sino Polis

31.03.2009

Today is a day like any other, he doesn't feel better, we'll sleep afterwards. Not knowing has always ruined many families but they understand me, they were not to say the mafia but worse. So you're lost, you don't know who to believe, who was that one where it's not better to go for a beer to forget, where are we? It's more what we forget, there's emptiness inside us, what should we erase again and then forever, our disasters? Even further down we don't understand what is there, inside the emptiness or not talking to have an expression anymore. You have to die to Fascism, of false Fascism not to speak and denounce you. You can't say dead and killed because you're alive and well or, it's forbidden to say that you've overcome an evil in the ego, the artistic property is refined so you're beautiful. I also breathe and then I continue to breathe, believe me it's all true to get confused to find yourself. It was so low the ideological thought of today compared to what it should be, you need to recover the consciousness of everyday life, of what you don't know why it didn't happen. Who tells you, where you want to find it written.

Maybe nobody understood us, it's not in the lexicon you find but where you look, try in your favourite drawer. Everyone defeats an evil, convinced in the fight then lose themselves are cheaters, beheaded your fans or your bosses. Here it's all expensive instead, sign good and original then you do a bit 'who, as, when so much will be inhabitants in the same place also mine. The weight, the smell, the obsessions the phobias to hope for. Today's massacre is nothing to them, they will always pay more or nothing for power, they are copies of us if you want to forget, while an insect should be taken as 'the best tool, better not waste too much but it is what does not make you speak well of me, wants to get into our heads convinced that no one sees it, to say it's a novelty. He will wait for the next massacre tomorrow, love dies, November who dies.

The classic is art, let go all those thoughts on your belly down on the desk, an exemplary cohabitation no or you are like that. The sea exists, what you want to know is what you don't know, plus where you were. Problems whose solution is obvious that you couldn't do anything about it, once there was nothing, he says, a time ago there was nothing but a surface, twice as bad, however, was what you say the pain. Here at my place there is no way to quarrel, those issues have already been lost, the solution is the way to go.

They will be sick people who are beaten, camouflaged to look angry, the words are in a non-compliant gravity, the error is circumscribed. Who speaks is the solution and still death, nobody says who or, what is the State, people do not exist is the topic of tonight: you have been erased, there is no solution is the easiest thing, because! by tradition goes along where there is nothing, the solution is you or, the streets have already been found, you are the object of what they are talking about.

Evil is honey aim too low your gaze, there is no more living space. Usually we are already in good or it all seemed to be over like tomorrow, where still coming is never back, it would be better to say it was wrong, tomorrow does not shine of any mountain but it is life, the way that arrives and then we are still in evil, still words there is nothing more to say or those files that have been deleted along with the many impediments not to make them say it again, it is human however they work in that point there, where it has never been possible, they would be instead those things that do not accept an off. What a dark night is here, the destruction at the end of the sentence, who was offended, who had to be and what had to happen. Now I tell you, nothing follows calm down, it's all the problems, it's days together as you see now or in a dream always the questions of the other time, you're still listening or maybe you got distracted, period.

After a while it's all over, it ends here, someone keeps silent about the act that you shouldn't have done or the things that they say uh, we all know for sure but the soap is who, not me or someone else. Even today of these promiscuous promontories of me perhaps you have already understood, you are the rest of me, you who do not speak or do not exist. It was all you had and you didn't take it, legions of humans have never lost anything of them, don't believe in evil but in its existence, I'll never stop to say it. It works like this: never deny your faith in God and chips, you're a boy you don't have a Synergy but only an Energy then, who will tell you how the sentence goes on: it's evil that speaks to you, that is your best friend, or who knows who will tell you because you don't speak with open A's. What an absence of state can do, nothing has changed, as five minutes ago a nightmare, so many things to tell you and life is full of mistakes. From sin one does not speak, a good thing how to get rid of the harmful part, explain what is said down the street, like a wall of cork attached to a part of the brain. Good and evil are like all things, they exist outside of you, around and inside. Your time with those you lose it because you are not there, you don't believe in good, you don't believe in a single wave form or a note, there are no free people while we are already an absolved neighbour. How many times we've been attacked, they still want to know what they're wrong about... thieves, scoundrels, those who suffer because they didn't manage to understand themselves even with a degree, they still want it because they're to blame or to get confused.

Here yes or no is the difference, the price for a life, the divine light reflected in the glass of a window, you've never seen a spore grow, still taboos and nonsense as eliminating the problem erases the source, it's just fresh air that costs as much as the source of happiness or the end of lies then still silences, curses washed by hand by the rain, in addition to what you had to do you build another. I believe in music not in mass suicide, how clumsy is the normal falsehood of humans, what you see! the strength of loneliness, of knowing how to be alone is much greater and longer, where they say I assure you it is false, the true is obscured, what seems oral is not words but actions against or for you, the irreverent fresh air memories of a wrong era already existed. Do you remember or have something to say about this, everyone says it's the past but, it's still useful today for something, so it must remain but, too strong indeed open is the wound, you won't even be able to talk, they never came to kill you quietly? Yes, you'll keep silent then, it's not the time of the past anymore, from prison they'll tell you how you can't call mistakes together with today's Sun or, that always the same wanted to pass for another, it's blamed on one who had nothing to do with it, you can't enjoy anything, tomorrow it's the same. Memories of the past, love, passion, music lost in time, plus wasted time.

You and me the power of your own throat, where the sea ends, as fascist as our time is, you see the light as it shines, and it's surprising to find your things at home in place, a little for everyone is so. *Bye G.*

5.
What changes

30.04.2009

"As the sea slipped away to find me out of a hole or a tunnel, there was nothing left to do."

Extinguished down there, as far as he said a thought to arrive, I suggest it had to be the wrong place, it's already finished. The place doesn't have to be a point to finish the places to be wrong, assess what the reality was, already look at the problems we have around us, they are always there no, and it's always a catastrophe from two millennia ago, who loses is constantly, who of course already done, people are living in poor misery. What will they then have to say to each other, how it continues even more decomposed or Alice is not there, you do not exist. Convenient products and fearful business of our low or other high countries, among other things what you want to continue, to do first. Where he stopped, I wouldn't know but I'm sure he'll have got lost down there in the background, near the bar or your favourite club, the law is where you go as always, even many people who are not employed in their jobs, too many free. The modern news, mechanics built on yesterday in writing to the judiciary, on posters in the municipality, the news are not really or completely so, it is a mistake to lose what already exists to see something else. You need an instruction on what you will see later, it is the school that still do not give, then another world is all well covered with a truck tarpaulin, like those who hit us with sticks, even the graphics are forbidden in this place that is not you but, a concentration camp. Uninterruptedly complaining until the point where it ends, while you know or you don't know, what or why we go, we advance as you see there are others there, I'm tired it's not even time to write to you: here those abuse is so they say to exist or to stay.

A product is never perfect, a white line for her as a rule is good, only if widespread is common, as if you turn off. A communication is necessary for what was the real act or form, a thought that does not express itself, you said the same with your participation. Look at the life I spend here, you there, television, business, so millions of people all for us already, the explosive quantity not the quality. What it means to have or live, engineer rings the bell all in their places, we leave. Note: the bell is fine the rings no, just today. When you don't speak, how much is it because already too much, too many people speak then, who for you, for me or for others, what and for what. The eyes are watching us, objects are thrown or that culture that doesn't take hold. You hear the sound of an airplane or have already seen too many transformations, look at the life that I spend here and you there. Peace is Easter you like to smoke or talk, I have already had three glasses of wine, after all there is a lot of work to do, someone has already understood me. Who lives with an evil or who criticizes a good does not exist, a thought is also what you, well is according to justice in its form, in its colors, what today may seem like a dream is really another.

You live but where ingestion or hiring are free, so many limbs are a little difficult, the days spent thinking, walking in the streets. Zero evils are to begin to breathe our time, you will see the world slip away like a wall collapsing down.

The verse is you, the church had been banned, serious problems such as forceful blows to the head and body that forbid our peace. Time is the key included in what you can say, there is no presentation in this state of those who have words, but if you want you can find many problems on the street like yours, mine, or if at home they deny the good these powerful artificial elected however is not true, as we were never born, indeed it must be only a success or, a new what is today. Good is a particular nature, not a concentration on the vilified object, where it goes exists without harm, not at some point just the public affair such as the question of having been reversed or guilt.

It was the month of May when it happened, people decide the future and the past, death for you, for me I don't know what to say, whoever kills the present is here, whoever speaks elsewhere only says the false. The usual evils without telephone, the day that everyone wanted to raise the title that is different for everyone. Turn on the radio is already history the rest of the hour, it is true that there are not many words that are needed but, why is already destroyed all our future with all our problem. Good morning, the air is not art. All 'success already happened, here it will be. It is the absence, the emptiness, the home tortures, the absence of state or laws. Yours or mine, what is it fair to say: where were you? You don't want to understand what was necessary or who speaks at the bottom of the soul, how many pains not to be alone. You see, the truth has already passed, how hard it is to write instead, everything is already old while the law still cannot be kept at home, for us or for that obstacle that makes us beautiful after understanding and overcoming it. I hope in your reading you will always want to put something of yours, so that we can understand the roots, how long is the river that does not want and will not stop. Maybe they didn't understand me, I don't want to kill him, he's already dead.

You want to know your school lineage came to visit me, I don't like to do everything myself but, a wound hurts, you have to close it also or above all by yourself, as sometimes to exonerate yourself from practices for a day from the invented Sun. A few moments or minutes are enough for a total resolution, and you do not know who you are talking to because it is forbidden to say, kiss or better to overcome. Only taboo boredom or deficiency, if not here what they bring: to make mistakes where the error does not exist but, for heaven's sake how come it is all hidden, so today reveals our argument that outrages us or, as everyone has preferred to continue. A charge for the day, that of... you know it always depends on who speaks of the time, of the era you live in, on your state and the democracy that and in force, with its laws installed, the losses, the lack of knowledge that passes through the brain, down in the street or on television, plus that strange business also associated with total resolution, it is curious then I am total. Keeping intact is today's practice because yesterday it was, how much confusion just as soon as you wake up today. Since then you have felt a memorable silence for ten years, not to mention more, they were sileni brand of torpedo, weapon used to turn off your house.

Humans come out of evil, this from the verb evacuate, people close to you, so things that exist around you, once they were warriors, now there is the problem of hunger but this is also a fact of the past, you arc always looking for a private place to breathe freely, there are those who want to bring the whole nation.

Listen to some music or, rest at a certain time you do before. Transform yourself that 'the world has changed, for me it's a crime to say something like that, right is to say the world has changed, now you're there go on. It's always a new, and it's always available sometimes changes, only one point disappears if you want in the world, that insult that nobody cleans up, in the sense of washing with detergent. A happy worry today, an email is a gutter. Where the sea ends the earth begins, this is not our common or two nations, but they can only be defeated by the laws of the state. Geometry and architecture tell us how the one who speaks is evil, the absurd division of houses into evil, then that where the state ends I begin is worse.

Ok so your friend stinks, this like the idea of where we live but, it's already true. Police halt, what do you think! Good morning, do you want to continue on which side, see at your eye why don't we talk about it, what happened to you in the afternoon, where is your state of arrest, look for the law state of arrest is report or lawsuit, on legal articles that force you to arrest, there is no one up here on the second floor.

Emptiness is our real continental threat, because it's not from here, or it's from here. In general it's the problem of being human, what do you want to continue, our city is empty then, that little problem comes back there is always like who told you and, to whom you made it understood. Too empty, you can't say the smallest words, a few moments from Sin city. False fascists, no holocaust story, feel the silence of the sulphur. How much peace it is to die today, how much duty one cannot and, other problems. Who steals, who plunders there must be a mistake, the State is not there, will continue tomorrow. The slogans, two points. One shot then the fresh air, a new atmosphere, new colours already, please. The dead who die without state, without blame. The arresting blow, whoever wants where he goes is unable, if I understood the limit, the threshold plus twelve or thirteen other things, to tomorrow which is always another day.

Life continues on roads that are not stained, even where we did not expect to go, fresh, perfumed by our free thinking, where I do not tell you who, you cannot say the name, cannot, where today has ended. A war that continues in peace, words cut out to command you not to speak. A law follows what has been distorted, or, what is stronger. Where good has ended, good does not end, even if we do not know where we are going, because we have fog in our heads. The subject of today is always the today that has not been, to go on without cuts, without blood. What you're afraid of has already happened, normal is what you didn't expect.

Fresh air, we are all tired, the perfect revolutionary, overwhelming ideal is not an abstract but, a qualified to repeat. It exploits the work of evil as a wrong software dearly, as to be avoided in the discourse of our actions. Poverty will never be enough, already the one who identifies calls you for his responsibility. Tell them what is missing, out of nowhere there is nothing, out of where they are installing there is only emptiness.

A hug G.

6.
Mercury, you and I

31.05.2009

"Help! the human who reasons, governs says today is better than yesterday. It made me laugh, among a thousand of those things I don't have time for. Ah, to think it over."

A confusion in today's question or the other, inside a glass. Too many things you don't have, too many robberies, a wall attached to the front of your body, too many needs. Who doesn't speak is yohur blood drunk in my glass, the saucer (small plate) was never foreseen as a Peugeot of memories, thank you.

A star is not just a revelation, it's outdated ignorance. The point where your code that's not yours or that thing's bottom or over there, who is it?

What matters is whether you're off or your political social system. Democracy, your real. What can't you, where's the fake or, who? These are non-natural architectural partition walls. There's no solution to that problem, you can't go out the door, where there's no door. What you wanted to know I know, leave those triangles only serve to avoid going back to where you were before, and you are no longer there.

What others want to know, that freedom that opens up where you were lost, and that was the solution or your misfortune, you can't talk about what you don't know, tell them no then it wasn't what, there's a massacre down the street, it wasn't a dream who the rest of your life was. You go out and you find what you felt, you come back and it's who or what they tell you is you, it's you don't know what, as you see we're always here. Those openings lose because there are places where even people are things, no more souls but objects to describe. Except for the guillotine, the loser is already there to collect. Who is more powerful enjoys it, isn't it? then someone will tell us what this function is about because here it tightens, end but still it's daytime.

It's then, and then ... a song by Mina, you start however drastically you walk, in the general sense of the words that we miss, the present in another word that we miss, good appetite to you too. Happiness in things that don't exist is where to remain silent, do you still believe the words do all those things they say, I think there is a wrong party to go away from but, the humans who think about it where are they? It's not all wrong here, ripped and thrown away forever. It's a little bit that interest from five minutes earlier, the not so you say. Did they come to you for evil? Ah, maybe your words don't come out, your fears or, what creation can give you, they stole you where it ends because you don't know, creation is easy. Being yourself in everyone and in everything is difficult but they threw me away, then go and see the millions of people thrown away, we are not a mine, each one where it ends but to whom you had to say it maybe I'm writing to you, you have to leave the back progress in time and hours, the future of not manifesting what you are, here is a huge variety of things, already but where you start a you know, or what is the bass, from the we are all alive not as it says extinct or black and white figures still. Goods or evils, choose souvenirs or caste, live better or still believe in many words, leave it alone when one runs away is out of breath. A picture of a sunny day that crushed the summer, the limit of where you cannot look because it is too high, you need the personal ownership of your interest in addition to the voice, the ideas that continue even today, what is not erased and is always in that direction.

An arrow between the eyes towards the front, it is the dynamics that vary, a function in communication there is no such problem, on the other hand they say we all disappeared too soon. The good doesn't stop, it's not the world outside the house, in a few hours so different. By the way, someone has basically done it, better another coffee! only five minutes have passed now they will continue their supreme strength. Theme: the demands of a day like any other, is wrong to talk so the mistakes are many and, the solution is far away, the voice goes out is not it? too coarse is to say that no one takes you where you talk. The animal that destroys is not good, the deposition of art overwhelms us, the day for the false.

The error is in adapting a society to that other perhaps imaginary society, you need to be careful especially if you do not talk about the points where a speech does not continue, you are seeing what does not stop or, it's just fog, it is not fascism to say this: for the distortions granted. The heaviness of a new day, the happiness of the time that goes on in the day. Millennia of sleep while in nature the solution is much simpler, there are other things, houses, those who steal no longer exist. Look, there's a bar over there, where they sell coffee, cappuccinos and croissants, the taste of bitterness that will ever be, hello boy.

Very important is who we really are, respect for others, what to do, where to go then, that we did not miss. Here make an X that says it's already all right where nothing happened, the astonishment of the thief or my uncle, Sinudyne or nothing. Panta rei, let's go back in ourselves, not the Earth travels without stopping. Sinudyne or Italy, everyone sees what they know deep down. Life has taken on multiple meanings from not being an evil, new forms, current ways of being to become, other existential types, open thoughts, acts, actions, clearer and faster permissions, towards horizons where man explains himself past eras, we know each other it is a matter of sweetening a little, in all those scripts that wanted our, theirs. It's a strange Sunday afternoon of dreams. He loves the repetition over the years of the same words, continue is if you cry you will know that evil is not a god, you see new horizons on the blackest silence. There will come publications of those ideas of ours or, configurations of eternity in past years then, look today not to think about tomorrow, who knows what it means has nothing to do with it, you have to head towards what you want to say, confirm everything is to note down in respect for others.

Here it is a routine where we also resist inside, to exist today where our problems end up, for me it is where they know not to die, when you have solved them let me know, they have been waiting for centuries. There is only emptiness, that is here // // (in evil). A situation can be different from what it looked like, we would have to close a little bit the State to discuss blame, crimes and limits or, why they carry a gun, we start from the phone calmly. It will be a good draft for sure, the poor people will laugh and, the rich ones as well, the topic will be: what had happened! Two floors of silence.

Goodbye, as always,
no hard feelings, G.

7.
The importance of clay

30.06.2009

Hello came June, a million thoughts and four kilos more Sun. Who doesn't say is reality as if it were truth, saying his name then is impersonal, you slander yourself or you contravene, you have to be offended to denounce him / her what you feel. Your myths don't say anything... it's silence, you don't know how to say why it's a mistake, you don't understand they already agreed, leave it where it is in the background it's ok, he studied, he has a degree, he has a job but he's a parasite of modernity, a caterpillar wants the ownership of the expression, then I don't understand how it's possible that the real things inserted in a speech are not said.

You have to be a nothing, not asking for freedom is a research? The others are for you too. A loss, illness are a bit different things, how come nobody says things as they are, because objective realities as well as a panorama can be not evident.

A stolen expression, mistakes, submissions or simply not talking for fear of making a bad impression. A because in the general sense, you have some ideas beyond. Fear of being hunted, a loss leads anyone into evil, you need to know how you want that public work, how many negative developments can arise from an unspoken thought, a society full of cracks you do not want to restore. Today words are few and far between, just impress them in two lines, what happened today, what was possible today then, what was yesterday. I know it always seems the same where the right ends, who is the strongest, who wins, who has overcome, we do not understand where we are and if we are identified, what we should not accept, there are things that cannot be accepted. What a confused time, too wide seems to me to be called the loss, always the same things is when it will change little badly. Looking me in the face is the solution to most questions, the contact.

The differences are many: I already know, the voice, the amplification of C. Well, what happened was not yours, you do not know the law occupies this place, there is no one there, right? Good morning life changes, whoever talks to you says the importance can have a useless, who is a null but can have worse axioms and copies of us automatically, who are then human for those functions concerned, have a salary and a machine. Shocking then, it will always be so, always the usual things is a matter of calm the ether, to bring to light we have forgotten today, and we complain about people who do not speak, deaf dumb institutions and thieves. It's nothing we have happened, only five minutes a day we are an anti-evil, from falls down, the taste of a stolen life, a serious loss of values and colours, I am cautiously and perspicaciously for no. There really is a new world, an explanation for the problems follows, it is the reason. The speech of before is the lobotomy beyond remembrance, instead what bothers us is the thought of the false or, a simulator of yourself, if you believe me there is an explanation, it is already so much to say believe me, where you go there is nothing, the emptiness interests you maybe ... an evil awaits us tried to hit us but, who does not speak with the verb is a concentration of words, of thoughts where an emptiness has been created.

What you think of an experience is a certainty

for tomorrow or, something to forget, a gas chamber or diesel fuel. How many beautiful words are thrown to the wind, perhaps with the hope that it would be clean. Act more word, under what I could never do again. Ring the bell everyone in bed, tomorrow the lager, the unspoken or written words. There is something well defined, still connected, tomorrow will be bigger than today.

The knowledge of school or the rest of life, of where we have stopped, because we are our whole universe, everything to be resolved for us and in us, we are all the things we talk about. The desire to fly, the induction to crime, the word gets dirty in a few words you don't feel like talking or you don't have a mouth. The subject is now well known, the emotion is stronger than thought but only fantasy. Tell me how old you are and I will tell you who you are in this age of duplication that will end tomorrow, I evoke where a heart is destroyed by a thousand wounds and irremediable folds, we will one day be able to get out of this tunnel or, is life another well-known question in our Italian homes, increasingly closed, when you delay in the evening. What you see in negative, let it flow, like a film of a film that passes in front of your eyes without touching it, as if it were going downhill. The blow you felt on your chest is evil, it wants to enter, you have other things to say, wait for a good film. Having a word duplicator also means being in two places to overcome, if you say it you laugh: they are one of those outdated things that have not been understood. The most important people are overcome and the living ones are already dead or, under a stone, you suffocate where or when you don't finish a good word.

A funeral every day, the past has already been erased at ten o'clock in the morning, to continue off until the evening that preludes sleep. Here are the mathematics and history what is evil, that bunch of things you don't need to know because you don't understand, sorry but who wants silence. In jail goes the equality, in two you do not win the law, is something you have to explain or, where duty is a custom, that 'the poison rest in peace bother the words said in half or, you want an interpreter for ourselves. Eclipse forever is something else, not what you see with your eyes in lobotomy tomorrow, this and that or, the windows. The law is written on a book not on a person, loneliness is sometimes stolen from ordinary people to give peace to evil, they have no right to have it. The rest is to fill in a questionnaire like a quiz, the solution is instead the way that does not hurt, painless. Cancelled or crushed what a problem there is, living in a volume seemed good instead is something else, this also considered an evil that is not personal, just merge. People are the way described, they resemble the work of art that depicts them, much in people is a being described, defined, you do not understand the object in our days, in its light and its darkness.

It's in speech and words what you didn't want to let people know, the presence of evil can only be seen by how you present yourself, let time dry that wound. Inventiveness and art seem imaginary, they are instead the concreteness of the city, of how you already knew it. Try to find someone tonight, when it starts it's already over. You who know who you're talking to, try writing down what you think and the importance of clay.

Goodbye, G.

8.
ISO 400 Photography by CS

31.07.2009

"Happy August is a turbulent time, you know where that fuzzy train is going, I told you everything. Quiet here nobody's talking there are the cobwebs, remember the plot of this film."

What happened this past week you remember, you like to talk. Another film of misery and nobility, in the basic present life is a film, as if you didn't notice we're in another environment not normal for the declared costumes of hospitalization, as if you wanted to make everything go well. We must always declare the true and the false also to have a clear vision, we are not those people, who want is who can. What is real for you today, the past with others, what has passed by on your own or, that visual of a distorted mentality? but if you don't speak it doesn't clarify your thinking. I light a cigarette, it's not difficult what you want to know, then if you are thinking about who has the possibility to talk to God, you will have to explain something more.

An existence changes, it can't always start from the emptiness of a concrete day, if you want a past to connect us to a present, a reality builds us, or rather, what we have built today, what is all that where a parasite can get insidiously, the inconvenient tomorrow, isn't there a bad thing? Artists are the after tomorrow, in my opinion humans aimed to hide a good, to make it see higher than miseries. Today, as you can see, what exists today is nothing to underestimate, our problems are not to be overlooked, and it is tomorrow that they will be solved. Art is not useless, it talks, writes, paints, plays, dances is not wrong, it is if someone on high wants the function that now passes us by, it exists. The world is true there's no doubt, like the other planets, it's the right way of goods.

Time advances, it is to progress with your whole person if individuals fall, where you are not, but, still you do not want to understand where it ended, maybe those gentlemen you see on the left side of the eye have gone a bit 'for the light, a good does not care about those things, you have to be careful, careful deeper the wound is another matter, the more serious is what you have to undertake.

The price of boredom, the emptiness and then you would enter into a false, as an absurdity on earth remains the day. It is true, however, that you win a good thing, but yours without you they have not done it, it does not exist, when they want to do it they will call you too, uh, with them. Look, there are still problems today, see your face. I don't accept the form of evil, the solution is today.

That function that they bring us then is the same as the other day, the other year but, they bring it today, so it takes a different form and temporality than always presented, the problem would seem to be another dilemma but it's the same, uh, over the centuries.

Words, friends, base, bottom, high, other get dirty in that function. A problem does not bring it home as your own, otherwise you too will not exist, it will be an art form about existence in good, not imaginary or useless but rather discussing the forbidden, the hidden because what you learn changes day by day. We are one sip more, see and die cannot be like that, people first are like you, then maybe they are constantly changed is not corresponding to the good, the surprise is to see that they are all our fellow citizens and acquaintances. You need to get used to the other, so there are others and others who have to go, it's also called clear the desk, trained you do not believe in what you do not believe, or it is around you or inside you what is not there. You feel treated high from the noise of the scissors, you can't resist. You knew it was there, it's another place close to the one you adored, you thought it was unique your way to Christian salvation, it's then in synthesis what it was.

Stop, evil is not attracted. Too coarse was modern thinking, they improved it, now what you think will be a fruit, we do not produce law was so because it was decided then, we stopped because there were no more words, because someone speaks, below that is all already lived as in a recording of life, then there are two types of auto play are the past that you have already lived, of your past years. The rest you know why you don't call? don't you see how many people are involved in what he says, it was yesterday as it is today. In this state you should report these things to the police, where everyone is.

18.07. The price of a life including that of colour, he comments last week, what was to happen is already a good result. We are in a box of what should be, don't you feel a bit tortured, it was what I was. They are beings to be denounced the good is already now, as time passes, a higher life what we are entitled to as described to the public, accustomed to boredom, to things already lived and experiences of others.

Watch the Sun rise or when it is high in the sky, someone is the reflection of what you see in your mirror, the rise of life that takes us forward to the next appointment or, at the end of the day, not like last week said who pretends to be master and winner, who instead lost just because he started playing or, also because he is a delinquent, it may seem strange to you but really have not yet solved that problem, among the many people who talk about it among themselves, the solution is this look at my hand, not knowing the good is a vital damage, as what you have just heard around you, it is because we are in summer to the precise words in depth, because so much if you do not say it they will tell you to get over a matter, since they have never reported you will come and tell you in the way that suits them to take you away, adult things are said of which children do not want to play, how to live the life of others' diseases.

It happens today pay attention to those sacred mechanical blows that come during the day, in fact you do not understand and yet it moves, it lacked unreality as fantasy this State, when they were goods of necessity.

What happens you don't see it because it happened in a clear way, there is no common expression, a peace that takes you where an evil has made you betray yourself, still hate and resentment, you won't get out, it's not your life, look at it where you stop, who has made a mistake in his life now thinks he is someone else.

The emptiness is imaginary, I don't suffer here possibly, plus it's almost the same for everyone. Look what a beautiful river under the house tells us then, it really passes a tragedy for ice cream, outdated practices you know, breaking an egg to find out what's inside. An imaginary valve, a vent, the lack, leave me, lose me. Things that were banned last week will also fall into the rule, because you also look for two points in the past. Jupiter, Integrro, Dinne, Ginger.

A difference is the threshold of what makes you concrete, what exists for everyone is also where others pay. Constructions like cookies are typical of existences in evil, on the other hand it is a life where you have not paid, the imitation of you. Emptiness is an existence of passage to live without, no one will ever tell you these things because you mature to firmly believe that we will not exist beyond, we will wither of what is not there, do not believe that 'the most good is normality for all.

The evil they do to everyone, you happen to fail from embarrassment or insult, from business not concerning yourself personally in the day, why continue with whom and where today, it will happen to you if you continue like this, to make mistakes in person while you talk to us in front of us. Common mistakes, texts about them that instead could simply be eliminated through concrete certificates, such as instructions for use from a legal state.

There is no written documentation, then it is also horrible 'the rest, buried in the house is perhaps only for your criminal record or, your bank account, you should go back a moment of twenty years you are a little' outside, you do not recognize yourself, it was already all wrong communication software, where you see a mistake that does not exist in the imagination, was perhaps a part of freedom. When the Italian taxpayer of this planet wakes up, how many injuries does he have? don't laugh about the fact that they can't be solved, how many sores are solved, how many years have passed, running out. On this festive evening, even if it's far away, I'll leave you a glass of orangeade and, at the end of a speech: leave that strange taste is better, leave it to those who want to say it and us to the silence of the music, of the heat. In person in person, in person to person how this speech continues, which one, who has lost, who has won in the end if everyone goes. Your business, the business of those who live above these things that are repeated, they hurt the heart and mind. An unsuccessful dream, look around to see how many people are not on that side, even how many outside the speech. It will change this sign as 'the time of a season, our time and our air. Besides sometimes you go outside, dear planet Earth.

I like the sea as the sunset approaches the evening of what you don't know, you still think that people only change in personality or that they are no longer there. Maybe you've cut yourself off from what better subject to think about it, it tells you the weather was prettier your eyes than when we were young. You see today how many problems, how many human beings, like works of art thrown at us, slip into us, some ask for personal vendettas, others imaginary. A power game, an abjection for what remains of us, then to discover a state of deprivation, fascist imprisonment, death and misery, degradation on people's shoulders. Come to Calabria you will see it is the same as in

Piedmont, you will discover that all this silence is misery, weakness of mind in general. A social degeneration like yours, years spent in silence suffering an evil to bear, to keep inside and then all fantasy. There are practices, medicines but you will live better you have to accept it, yes because even good things are to be challenged or discussed here, mental closures some strong and lasting other mild, in general you cannot go out much, someone says there is but, push out even with difficulty black magic. That object just passed through there you see how happy it is, outside it is without conscience, you have fun in the background is however in practice really there are those odious forms of parasite that attack on you, they wanted to take you too, to take you away from hell. Really then how is the water you can turn somewhere else, is to see the future and people, pause. Look at what's more than a mistake, it's a blunder.

In these modern times you should be careful with this idea of not accepting the good, that problem must be denounced as they have not yet done.

You see what's happened, continue that river...
memories, end G.

9.
We are not those people

31.08.2009

"We're not those people who come from your unused paperclips, you have other things to say, so what's going on today? the economy, work, you don't talk is you say absolutely nothing."

Here we are not those people, in the end so we begin we are just ourselves, prose or poetry. You still have that doubt, certainly dear but it is a mistake, a sea of inaccuracies that odeo made. The road ends there, where you don't know who you're talking to, it's like I told you in the past call a lawyer. Life is not a flower that ends at ten o'clock in the morning or after two hours, it always continues, as you well think it's already solved that serious problem by law, which has never been used, never been, never been used.

If you ever knew how deep that hole-well is in the year we live, even if I warn you it is still full of perplexities, that is, full of evils. In five minutes you explain it is peace in your death in life, that is forbidden to think, that is what you mean. Doubts, many jobs to do, fears, how much money is missing in your bank account, believe me you have to make your own favourite rooster. It was time for change, better to sing in the morning for that other joys that take away our time, excuse my youth.

Valentine's Day everyone is what you want, if you look at it well, but it's strange, different the only day you haven't lived in silence. It's better to dare to know without any doubt, only if you follow it continuously would have been a good solution, we would say goodbye for the moment to a part of all those problems, if we had to know what we mean by everything but, in the meantime, I'm here and you're far away that the world was still as far away as its light. Still today how much strength to arrive at evening, it seems different, this oblivion to honey, applied to life, is greater than us. Where is what one believes is still unresolved, on the other hand one often remains without reason, if one has to be swallowed up without even knowing who or what to make stay. An opening in the earth divides us from a very long time, to forget about us or to forget the solution, or to leave us full of parasites. Mistakes that overwhelm us are not allowed, they are not true then, it is life afterwards when it comes to what we are, it looks like a photograph, tomorrow will already be yesterday.

In important things the end of what is scary or nauseous has happened because of what seemed right, where a moral ends or the person will be precluded from saying it or, you cannot even whisper, as today we are on vacation, the blame is in the past year, not the worst is yet to come, the light makes things shine by themselves their simplicity. Without prompters we live better, we are left with only the gnoseology of a past life. Who we actually imagine, the silence in the words of our neighbour, I wanted to make you understand an existential cut, the price of our dreams, is of a freedom sliced the rest of us that continues in other people.

Who's talking? Where do we start from, how strange is the light of the Sun, how beautiful it is or Sun and Naples, make a mistake in person under the counter and then make us stay alone. Connect it is no problem, press the switch and say I didn't do anything, even a non neo-fascist symbol is enough. At the beginning of a relative reality you can't say what you can't say, do or kiss, swearing is a game for the inexperienced but, they always remain closed in evil.

Shut up you can't talk or concretize on anything about what sticks to our natural thoughts to stay more than five minutes in the days, maybe who now thinks wrongly that he had already done it. That little dot that you see in negative then it should be you who have made a mistake, less sky than nothing, already felt what does not make us grow ... stay still for the smile of others. In evil is like a misfortune of Dante that takes us where our hearts are sorry, and there is your window shame of oblivion, because you continue, I am tired.

We have what we can afford, in this world fruit of secrets never revealed, necropolis of humans sleeping awake, functions not resolved in a parallel materiality that nobody says clearly, we do not realize how much infinite misery there is around us, people are duplicated by others, falsehoods and guilt in crimes. We should remain bad, a fake, a photocopy even if it works. Someone never uses the world, it was just a bad nightmare but you have to be careful anyway, at the bottom there is the sea, you never know. One summer day at the beach, who has finished life? work is always a lot, look at how many people, how many needs, the dreams of young and old. You have the intention of today dear throat cut, the unknown loss of consciousness, the typical Calabrian mockery widespread elsewhere. The functions must be told us those too, you come from a desk of silence? wait five minutes, look at the future what you want but, not my girlfriend so as not to disturb. Today people deal with their disturbance in its various forms, what starts again, who starts again, who wants, what they want. She somehow has memory, two flowers for your interest, fan or star.

In such a living prison, as a state of abuse, there is no connection to speak with one ear. One uniform tube in too many equal, few state uniforms or, lifelines. Listen to the past where you live or do not live you pay, you calculate everything with precise measurements, exactly the same people. What I wanted to tell you is duty, patience, measurements, distance, what never ends, where you never have to put your hands. We are not stationary or, still life, we speak, we act for good, not actions or calculations of others, unconscious or uncertain. Listen to your voice even in prison, give it your form of stasis or the strength it takes to speak of great absolute problems. On the other hand we can't stop, it's the evil that wants to enter, it's the lack of respect, it's the brain or, it's the gas, uh, the gas oil. The story starts like this forever, many things already exist have a name, a quality is a peculiarity. The freedom you want to travel with you, always keep yourself informed, even better than keeping fit, or you are one of those people, that's why they arrested you end the phone call.

Good luck, G.

10.
My good is the good

30.09.2009

"All that is ours and all that is yours is normal. Build an artificial music: how much it costs to love a silence. "You say what's right for you, dying has never been easy."

The next line is empty, so begins the sentence to get out of a silence without using an evil. We leave sometimes not to arrive, as in the sea you can't see the end, the shadows play like ghosts, they attract me with nostalgia and sometimes fill me with emptiness, it's useless to start with the things I could have done, we have never gone beyond a life because we are tired from the labours, destroyed by years and emptiness. Some people smile at my uh, our misfortunes that present us as their fortunes, those who have the right to speak about us, those who vilify in a bloody way, they explain that they are a friend or, an acquaintance, but the road is one, then I am your light even while a futuristic fascism, the baroque of nothingness is still advancing, we are buried in forbidden things. Tell me who bans furniture full of light, real objects to replace the self-denial in the false. The beautiful words or the illegal, the power led, who silences good people to give, to feed the criminals. They are those people and you do not know, do not be afraid to express yourself remains acquainted because the error is disproportionate not knowing the word, a much more serious than what it says, you did it.

In the end the reality is out of the house but, it has never been easy, the precision is acquired with practice and people are always the same. Accept reality, who speaks to you or who wants to exploit you again, even 'next month, after is instead the completion of all the things that exist put together, to create the modern and the present different from all time. Many things on Earth are different in the eyes of those who look at them, for example misery where people of the law do not arrive or, as you cannot imagine how low those humans who do not speak compared to a living and present thought. You lose the sense of what is really important without seeing it.

Remember whoever you want, you don't have to give. At the same time a thought is right especially if written, today is full of insults for everyone, insults on thoughts and words, acts because of those who have to pay. Argue at the bottom and wide all the objectivity at best, as I do to empty that container, you need to be ready when it fills again. They were in function of what he wants to denounce you, tell me when is if still today, of a time where everything that lives today, can take back a value even economic that someone can overcome.

Here are too many filthy, to say the exact term, in oral communication, spread in all ways, the same always, the hearsay from people today, always the same evenings, it will be because of the echo then that you hear even if at low volume, someone has won but, still many fears, if you knew how big is your human or how large it is. They are so great the fear and envy that 'the rest of the diseases are them, infamous or sick even if at this hour I am not very interested, are the people, the diseases. Annihilate him or denounce you the opposite excuse, even if he must be a friend or an acquaintance of yours but he certainly is, otherwise you have destroyed the world along with an evil, the rest is where you go. You who know and do not know what, I tell myself or someone will never come here, it is the time you take, the time spent in an interval that create the diversity of words and actions to understand.

You'll come tomorrow, it's just phrases that end up where you can't go anymore, who knows what you wanted to say or other more important ideas, that I don't have time to list. Everything that is normal does not exist, let's leave it alone it's too late already for your only secret, what you saw today is already who you really are but the same as you can say about the forbidden, you can't what we would have already from yesterday! Turn what an ugly word, what do you think happened to me? they are infamies, you know that's how it goes on deaf mute. In 1759 the division of humans to live as free as they say since then without harm, is almost impossible in today's world. He asked you for money, here you don't pay, for that or that other business or action, the wonder of the light in the day associates our memories to the notions of science and culture while, huge swastikas on our heads tell us too many taboos but what then, these are evils as there is a great need for associations especially legal or artistic. Between past and present to move the arts, the bad figures are overcome, as you know things are overcome in the present, here are the malevolent ones. Who knows what he meant, someone is talking but the sea is too big. What are you preparing for tomorrow, what are you interpreting today, the diurnist martyrdom or a denunciation where is the office for the x's, it is necessary to relate the world's social product today with your own every day, the end of the world has already happened, even what you had to do in the next few hours has already been done uh, we have overcome each other among all in nothing, doing nothing. An air pocket like a thunderstorm, an earthquake, an explosion between elements that worked, never bring home the evil, Andy he or the other the last unknown words.

Look how tragic this reality was, where only someone speaks not to make a bad impression, the eyes were shiny with real light. If I could phone to say goodbye I would, if I could just say goodbye I would look at you but, our new-born love is already over. How capable is an if, free the day begins again, a nation full of friends and discontents, a comment on speed. What remains will be ours forever, we don't need to know very little, words don't get confused and it's true that it's enough but, it's not always possible to understand, there's always a need to be contemporary, how to see better than the folds in people. In its place, in step with the times, not only flowers in the meadows, continues who has courage but, careful where courage is not needed, continues who continues! Strange how the morning starts again or, a Sunday is particularly smiling, in those functions like the remaining subjective uniqueness's are upset, the clouds move. One of my theories about modernity says that we have already disappeared, a kind of over twenty years old. Choose a good, not false fascist fire of your own, so as to tell you which way is a good and, the others uninteresting. What you have lost, you don't have to look at it anymore, what it means there are no words, maybe someone was drinking a coffee. Indifference or gas chamber in this present of living memories are like garlic, say what is forbidden or, you don't want to know. Who lost? The answer is in the other room, who still wants to win in ten minutes a little tranquillity, many things are repeated and others are no longer repeated, as they do not even for the antechamber of the brain.

Remember, there have come to kill in the house, this is never said, once you have heard a person say such a thing. Another we give, it's not an element to say or confess, maybe it's because of that strange construction that moves only in our senses, that destroys the speech, that there is nothing. Tomorrow it will be a disaster, we should take care of it but who knows who, maybe we will go in a conjunction for a whole day uh, we are the most important person around us, we always end up like that, then others continue. The trick is that somewhere we exist, stop. Believe me if you suffer there is someone who understands you, or else it will be evil work, mystery and envy, reality is another day that has happened before. We still talk nowadays about where the error is, eat or eat, that 'good is superior to evil.

Everything is here not now okay, but not today nor tomorrow says who wants to shut up, so everything is always, always as many beautiful things are forbidden today or, how many things I have not told you, end.

Bye, G.

11.

Your clothes in the window

25.11.2009

"It's November those gender issues are still there, fortunes are candy. It's not possible where an insult begins, and for juries, technically what you want to understand."

The drawing is not visible but it is a mountain of idcal things, hiding behind the computer background. Whoever knows how to do these things is a thief, a drawing is there even as if it shouldn't be there. Barriers to the brain from age or the body, I say it will be more a matter of being us, so of being ourselves, or, in my opinion, who we are more than what we are not doing, existence is real, that is, in life. One question is whether you are alive for all things existing, today is a day, a mystery will be something forbidden beyond the taboo.

How many beautiful drawings there are everywhere, the Sun grows like every day, it creates hunger and light. Beyond here, everything is understood plus the word everything, the heart is like the echo of people who have spoken little, there is always something of yours in a bureaucratic social discourse, from the present depends what you want to understand me or, is what happened, from fear, distance or disgust.

A taboo is silence in institutions, vulgarity where there is redemption. Remember a calculator to do the accounts of this life, which has been advancing for two hours is between two occasions part, and then there is only waste, starting with the new, extras that fill the gaps of ignorance, the taste of fresh fruit. Beautiful Italy or the rest of the world, the border, God but who are we ... lost in how many years have already passed, how many more. How obscene it is to be lost, forced to bark, want a lawsuit or who knows what is convenient today, better to denounce those who take care of us, more than the cobwebs, you are afraid to stumble, you already know.

Anarchy is wonderful, too much is doing two things at once, a good is all together as if it were to seem or a chapter of history, culture in general, the horrors of humans solved all forever. It must come what happens, what people do or think at the shore, the light of the word is not our personal experience, you finish the sentence but, there are many hours left in the day. Sometimes we get lost in order not to find each other again, you know who is a universal language that doesn't talk about misery or an existing flirt. Everyone works where they say they are, everyone knows what you want but not that it's true, look they work hard because they are not there, that's how it is! On the other hand, what was a good only the future, if you talk to someone doesn't even understand you, because it's located outside and inside the rest, it's when you want a good, go and do to meet a definite neighbour and it's real. Maybe you did not understand, we do not have the text where it is written what is said, except this maybe there is no speech spoken by the institutions to people for those things because they were the pain, we are where the persecution ends that is called the right complaint.

Even today the Sun will grow until lunchtime, I pray from the path all the way down the gate, continue is not to persecute you. How many evil ones are there in every town and country connected, all in the same game. You don't understand it from afar, you don't change those things are the law, you bury them, you use them for food or you use them to the fullest.   Just don't cry, come on. Who booked? After all it was just boredom, plus it was where you arrive as you pronounce the action of your belief, I do, you do not even if we were treated badly let it be a prize there are more than eighty percent of existing things prohibited today, loneliness is everything but also a good thing you know, alone is easier to kill you or, hit you. The speech is over now continue your thing that grows in your chest you're still cancelled, answer who kills you today? You see we've found evil, it's nothing. Improper and other different objects are not coloured in current Italian, there's no talk of death for good, whoever said it, whoever speaks suspended dots.   The return of those who must be denounced, talk to those who have not told you your ruins. The true and the false, the salty and the sweet, etc. the contents are in other words.

Where did you go to finish that function again or, still your life, the quintals of your fat, you always have something to say, just, firm, soda that we are in Italy. Flying, arriving at a good thing is infinite, who you are is also difficult but you exist even if only to dissociate yourself from a doubt, instead everything is already over, it is already a triumph not to be left out careful. I already have the solution, you already know the explanation. A software or, a program instead of how it is without living here, they duplicate you to not believe that God is alive, there is much more for today's day than you could have, you need some eyes open even if a little crying, you know the rest ... tell me what I wanted to remind you, now don't tell me anymore. Always continue on that side I advise you to avoid the cold, those words that cannot be said, but only justify them are a trauma of consequences, professors, professions, prophecies and religions, we are there. It's a math out of evil, just can't be said, they are just school mistakes but at this time, two hours after lunch. I already have the solution, in two hours they'll kill me and we won't know anything about it. You know sometimes it is necessary to go back on the right steps to help us to walk the road tomorrow, we are the other word of what you refused or what they wanted to make you deny, you and your needs. Duplicating and identity theft, not talking about it is worse.

Time has served says the law, what you see is what exists where it was possible. Overcome the superintendents, ghettos and cats who later work in a public office, the recruitment where you were last week, you know how to recognize a state of arrest? Then they ignore each other, he's a comma, she's a ball. In operation is enough, it ends like rain when it stops, then who will be the art or the structure of human activity. What work you do comes back, you find what it was, what you left behind, you just have to get used to it. More complaints, look at the Sun as it spends differently, always. Continue is useless, you lose state and small good or you are the occult.

What they keep hidden from us is the preferred price, the concrete and other, all 'l paid with the taxes of the other month, good day at this public office, where our arm can arrive, cannot continue who is false or who has lost. The favourite dress cannot be living in evil as the devil or, a form of demagnetization of memory, so it is how you never get out of that problem.

You see that you do not see! and that's all after, what is a slow-motion is not the others to understand us. Well you have to be on or better awake but, our clothes will stay ours forever.

Bye, G

12.
Fantasy sometimes flies like 'the thought

20.12.2009

Fantasy flies like thought, the important things remain but sometimes they fade away too. Your problems nobody says there, you have to stop that mistake that the voice doesn't take care of. So vast is that traveller's question prolonged that his news comes to you, know you do not get out of this horizon then, they will tell you who you are talking to. We'll see another new day that arrives anyway, what's beyond that paper wall, what happened to you on the plane then, instead of not even knowing what you wanted, applause for Fibra, joke.

Everything is real, everything is subjective. What is the ignorance in whole people in their integrity, maybe they have to leave because they are too united, there are other objectivities that are needed, as if you are talking to me and you get lost with another person, see here is all your space. There is still a serious dilemma in this world, you who are engaged to what is a threat to the imminent danger of the Earth, later those who speak today do not want to be communicated, and it has already happened all the dear problem of the whole is true, as Jesus Christ was already put on the cross, already for many centuries.

Beyond that, you write that you run out of ink. The world and its colours cannot do all this evil, it will pass like a feverish illness while the same people will always be the ones to answer for theirs and for others, your good, good in general, your favourite information, struggles, internal and external wars, you come today in the progress of tomorrow. Sometimes it is useless to go on, with all the people who are there you have already understood it, you will have felt a tear or you are already those who have concessions to die, and it is better not to hear friends express themselves there, it is forbidden to talk about it. An example for those who want to be careful, it turns out that from the forbidden an evil wanted to be the devil, instead it was evil. It won't be long before lunchtime, what a confusion life is not dead!

In this December of the year zero nine, year dominions, they talk about the unmentionable as themselves, it turns out that there is no need to worry but, that we would not have solved that problem near a side as well as the work, the house, what is it that people say, who are you really ... at least so you understand me is not even complete, whole or real, legal what happened last week? Maybe you've heard of heresy or blasphemy, blasphemy or heresy in the future. You know they said the weather has changed but if you haven't received updates don't eat it too much, nobody says anything, it will be too strong the case.

The contact of the solution seems harsh, not cultivated, the cork is who you have to talk to, who governs maybe it bothers us, the fact that it is not possible to make it all at home by us then, there is still that problem, how it has not yet been resolved, indeed it will have become a retro progress or even a copy of the opening of their graves to life, the opening of their bodies, laugh who knows what convinces wait but, you do not see anything public. Today a new day begins, here is a new productive theme I hope you always understand me, we are above all and we stay here. Today is glued with glue to yesterday, now we continue what you want. Pay attention intellectually to what happens to you good, good work, what is finished today is really finished.

The insatiability, the endurations what flows in our bodies, in our blood vessels, today's humans are dangerous, that place must not exist, we shouldn't go there, then there is no need, it won't really exist anymore, they'll erase it, it won't exist anymore. School, work, marriage, we must also speak publicly, it should also be made clear that we need subtitles, how to sleep, ahem, rest, if they sold you, tomorrow buy yourself back, you'll see how different the reality was so different, is what a serious mistake in person. The job is your car, your alarm clock. Tell me, do you know what it means to tell me, what is that noise as you move your back, what do you say I'm louder? Tell me the people who woke up are not turned off. Say it I have not spoken, you see how deep the bottom is, how dark or, incomprehensible was yesterday's day yours too, write it on a sheet of paper and sign it: a past and a tomorrow will be the future.

Remember, the bread gum rubs on your head then, tell me all the goods didn't die with a gravestone. A darkness in the light is a thing that should be thrown away or left for advice, instead look at it continuing towards the end of the road without you, for ever and ever. You understand, of course you understand is today that other day where we are the winner of the lottery prize! Theme two points, hello Sunshine welcome back. You want to talk, continue because you laugh? you already have what you want to open on the basis, so deep down the bottom you do not see it but, you know what because you know what you're doing or you did before we met, it will all be useless from you write it now, power is the game of those guys there. Surely you'll have trouble spreading the bones of your body, it's him who's tight. The end of the world, the end of you, it's not over, over is another year. A window is all the universe you could expect, a to be continuous, but you are the biggest dilemma there, do, re, mi, there. You see how high the Sun was, from this you can consider how low you will be today. Wait, wait, wait, it's over.

Happy New Year, bye G.

13.
Maybe you want to listen a little

03.01.2010

Dear friend diary, beloved friend I exist, I'm already where it is yet to come. Start after a coffee, the other words will be written in another book, maybe the one above the table. Convenient, tell me another word and it's already over, maybe my older friends than me did not use many words so to speak easy, to say the same things that serve today not to go wrong but, we are the destruction of the false. Who was supposed to come? after what was supposed to happen in this year zero ten did not do it, they seem innocent, they did not achieve anything, not even the desire to say it, you know who had to support or how difficult it was, it was not the time from how many mistakes were made.

A human access is happening to him uh, you as you know Mr. denounce or, the end of silence. Who doesn't light us is a right monthly income, you need to realize how many things were not done, even by their large number, or you need to observe our flame modified with a different brand.

Fascism is not a child's play, it must be forgotten or remembered, here write it down on that book, is continue on your way down to its goal or, Mecca. This was what you could expect, you don't know: the end prefers your person. Calm down here nobody knows, even because of the time you spend on that side or, on that known side. The others are not fakes, they are others, what you wanted, what you had to be or do, others will make it, while you will be yourself, without your close beings. No one here knows anything, just the wrist.

How deep is a torn pain, how right the law will be, in the night hours do not trust the action is after the move. What exactly did you see, who advised you, because it did not happen what you expected for you and the others, I tell you the future has not changed, has not been improved, on the other hand as you see is right next to you the dagger that betrayed you, suffocates us that someone says anything or, a phone off. The future already knew it, good digestion, there is a heart of movies on television, do not tempt me to the dark side, then you recede where you did not want to believe us, you need to be careful with those who speak in our days, it is clear and clear as the morning frost our being, it only works in that sense or towards, in the name of verbal voice work for the true, even if you do not speak.   Tormented by submerged worlds while there are goods, what is already alive where we will be, you will hear today in the centre as exaggerated, now I'm going to get another coffee, another I understand, here's a break.

The communication is gone, maybe you want a story or a fact that makes you understand better, it's a good thing to tell at the beginning of this year but, the exaggerations are expansions, swellings like tears in the throat and the thought, towards where it was not even possible to see you again. To say the least, the nineties, eighties, seventies and sixties will have passed, their revolutions are paid with state benefits, to finish a new year begins that is death not tasting, not the awakening of what it means us, look at this wrong sky of problems sitting next to us, then I think the air is difficult to understand, that horrible confusion, that torment that agitates us, do not sleep on the mistakes that have made life missing right under the house or around the street corner.

The favourite citizen is as they say the grease on the fire, maybe you were waiting for a precise drawing of what happened or, of how you want, relax, melt, it's the air that burns that unresolved function, what is called your impending error. What do you like, what is the cure to absence, your favourite perfume, you are no longer you, the world has been overcome, tell me why nobody solves the question already solved in the document that was the world and people, from big to small there are always the same problems, you will understand then that it has not come to someone, to us alone, ourselves nothing.

From what has been known have modified some series of personal certificates by not inserting compatible products in the right place, listen to the air is the best perceptual tools of many centuries, who dies is the fish. Your problems are state not yours, the past is not erased, remember what you were doing now is who you are, what was possible has already happened, what will happen for the rest of your life is all described today.

I'm tired you want to arrest me? Don't swallow that stuff, who are you dating? Don't worry about anything anymore, life will always be better. Burn me because I'm alive, you'll be late and early. Our rhythm, we're alone don't go crazy if you succeed, look how many walls. Our daily constraints disappeared together with the most powerful of spirits, you can see and you can't see the mistakes of yesterday, it's you who had to go bad today. The mistakes of an entire year, the mistakes of a nation that doesn't look at another.

Hello year zero ten tries to go for good, the good. The flowers depend on what colour, you have to see if there are thieves on the leaves or, on the branches then where are you? how many walls in what year two thousand and ten we are. Try to go to good in this state of persistent, existing, present sleep. It's your business not to say anything anymore, it's Saturday, it hasn't been decided yet if we are a woman or a man, it will be a general function that you say outside the walls of the house, you already know that you're not there, you'll never succeed because you're not, after all you can ask but, many things you can't know, it's not polite to know the next one. Bad word polite, it's better to say: sleep when you're awake so you understand me.

Chimeras and crystalline ornaments, honourable mirrors of your existence, what they say, better not to talk to sugar today, in a state of arrest on the beautiful. The more someone has to know anything, the more it doesn't have to work, the girls are happy so it doesn't work! it's better to blend in and disguise yourself, it's not necessary to talk about the hatred of the city. What they say, I don't have to hear it, uh, not even you, but it's a war that has been going through Italy for a memorable time, now the tree that wants to stay comes home, you always have flowers for those guys who want to drink, another line, another question, just that 'the bus passed by and I left, do your good where it tells you, where is that wonderful story, there are many of us in the world but, just a few words are enough to make sense, see what they wanted and who! Another line is you're not even there anymore, from school explanations then, spend your life redoing the accounts and then find yourself old.

Bye smile, see you soon,
too many things, G.

14.
Beautiful, playful floor

01.02.2010

Today is Sunday... maybe you know your main problem: what will happen to the others. The trouble of those who were stunned when they saw the good today at this hour...

I repeat the words, I feel dazed, one solution is that from the beginning the day could not be done because it was impossible from the moment you wake up, make your best changes. What will have happened the other year, the state where it was was not really an I, I'm not the one who has those problems of now but, it's already a dilemma to be yourself as having an ID, even if I'm not your favourite singer. Here works your dream next week too, yes you are good but there is no State today.

The dream, uh, where's the reality? Go out into this filthy world what fantasies you are or, if you want better extirpation. You want a future? You're gone! What happened today how come? How can you say twice how.

Big business around us, you treat others by looking at the people around you, what you did wrong is you who know, the world is big, the money. They are your mistakes, don't split your head in half, I think you know who they are. It's cutting that knife in the daytime or, in the evening seen presented again today, already better: we don't know each other but, you should be me. You stopped because you're crying your sorrow then, it's one of the goods you shouldn't have today. O state who is your state? because someone says things to your face, those things you wanted and you didn't have. A void is a drag? Past things or things of nothing, they say but we are not a colander, all right, see you soon.

Don't say you did wrong, you didn't report a wrong. What do you know when problems are bumped off, today what you live uh, lives. Must be all these things we were already, what's best for you is you're not there, since all this is good. What good? Laugh ah, keep walking here is all bad, after the future is a gunshot. Still your he or she burns, since the times that run, your she/he burns, the world burns who knows where they will have found all this fire to life. Using water for your costumes does not suit me, believe me, these rooms are two-roomed rooms, graves in the house, what are you afraid of the future, you have never been in the future. Who lost? Nothing is the answer. The secret of the world that continues in evil is silence, if you want explanations call me later at Easter or next summer, if so continues no one speaks, no good, no sleep. How many explanations do you want today, who is someone else hasn't understood, how many will you want tomorrow because he thinks that you have lost patience and you don't want anymore.

The will starts from the stomach, he didn't understand as Carmelo Bene says, who was also the one who spoke badly. The information passes like a square connected to the brain to create another tomorrow, always alive unfortunately for those who are like us. When you look at an advertising board you believe in it, natural light makes a new day, hunger or something else, it denounces itself by living and suffering from glory and peace instead of blue, it and then a little bit further on a fruit. Ten years ago they won't have understood me, already with a lot of effort in your stomach you will be able to declare the truth, Italian boy, dear well look at your friend, maybe the illustrious colleague, collaborator, dear state will have escaped. Tomorrow they will take another to do the Good, maybe our former friends will have toothpaste in huge quantities.

After many passages of time they will come to my house, the publicity will not, they still try by irreverent act and action. You have to talk with your mouth about how we are not interested in the grave and in life, a main policy is look at these people, more than anything else they are to be cremated, if you have the science of government, the law says these days that he is so wrong for real, here you can say what you want, only you do not even know where it is. To tell you the truth, there are too many Sigmund Freud, problems in the fan, worries to discover, why are you infected? You're infected talk, nothing doesn't answer, you see how evil stuns today. Eh, how many things you didn't build last year, while you were doing other things.

"You're the one who thought there were no other things to do today."

Remember your past, go through it better, let go of those negative hypnosis with all those things that are not yours, wave goodbye with your hand even to Mr. head and son complaint, if you have unknowns comes after you get into a fault then, you see the typical Calabrian friend like a fig, his particular smell, gratitude two thousand and four: I did not want to apologize, bye guys.

Up, above, here's the north now you also see 'his particular colour, blue, anti but, think of the future you do not understand the good. It was believed that we did not eat creams like zabaglione and zuppa inglese which is very good, it is not him or her ... must continue another unit that is not me, maybe you or another then those on that side of the crystal, here I have to get up the obligations are still many outside my room. A butcher's shop, a haberdashery is already what will have happened to all the people in the world, you want to go out and take a look as it continues, how it goes, go is the law that governs your absence then, only part of what should be later, I cannot talk to you to tell you what is your favourite cut or, the bad and unworthy jobs already built. It's you who will go on, the pressure and so on, oh God what misery and/or falsehood, we're just one by one, singles. Praise to the guys who got distracted and have already overcome an evil, what was this word evil, the echo outside the house of things are not yours, who wanted the freedom to go, someone says it bothers them and remembers those occasions that defame the taste. Adrenaline is preferred no, a dark voice says stop dying, it's so subtle what do we need? are your habits perhaps dark, even if now you run away you go in the strangest directions only above the ear, above a hand, chest, a leg or both legs because he did not understand you. Come on, you don't look ahead you see it's behind, because it's in jail, ahead there's only who and what is said ahead, jump leave the hole where you are and go for the next one. A solution for our little life will be open to many solutions, it is one like the road that takes you where you want to go but, here we are all alienated for our society, drowned in coffee some are with you but, what does it have to do with it, it was out of function because the problems are from the past to today, what are we really? they seem to me a property like a holy field.

Today you laugh again, end of speech. You repeat our product, everything is real what it really is, so a product is to go everywhere. How much futility and waste of time do you not believe, we are the greatest killers of ourselves. That's yours, that's useless how good it was today, who ruined it or, what will ever happen to you. Who is the intruder, what is your nationality, after all something is eating at you, long live the Sun. Two words about your empty friend, then bloated with air: please good afternoon. In short, all my life is extinguished when I go to sleep, the words I miss! The problem was what I had to do today could not someone do it, yesterday instead will come tomorrow, while the other year will come tomorrow or after tomorrow. What don't you know about me, all state failures but, don't go to someone's house because nobody solves them.

Say what you want, shoot your continuous flow into life and earth or, your main question of the year more you don't even know who you're talking to. After all you remember today what could have happened, look at him still laughing is the theme. Must be problems of the State, good evening remember, it's been a long time, that is three days are not our business? The time that stops, the time that is not yours, you see your ruins, the window of my house is tell me more time to lose, to spend, who wants us steal us or, the lobotomy is who you really are. Your good is not true, it's only an evil... how low is our Commune then, just those who tell you that you are an evil are them as they say the not growing up, on the other hand then is our baseness or our age that finally guarantee the unripe to the original life, to the true personal retrospective. We will see how many things we are forced to know in order to live in a concrete way tomorrow, and why we are forced to explain the position on our own and not on our own. I've always liked to write about sleeping at night.

How many accidents you have, why haven't you finished? What did you want, who the mighty, the rat as you soles, you grieve. You see our problem... some accuse us because we say ours anyway, but it's a heavy absence, no offense, no offense.

Bye, G.

15.
Bananas

01.03.2010

"Classic tobacco, nicotine to smoke on the way to your favourite spot, even if you don't say we're in a busy, full period, full of prohibitions and bad advice."

Another proposes his eyes to understand what cannot be understood, it is difficult in its simplicity the error of a false fascist as it is difficult to understand who he is. Emptiness, nothingness, not believing.   He only renounces the way we have said the same in the past, you can see up to this year back in time, you find me the same, my classic tobacco, the property at the bottom is out of a cardboard box. The classic is the property of a private interest! In the most general sense, what is meant by the broader profile of objects. Ruin of the classic is what is going to happen, what today as we study is said, everything but not for life the discourse of objects continues, or rather a real person can be an article. Our inappropriate today, good words also serve to concretize, how to treat an object throughout its entire length. The evil, however, has already been defeated, all that remains is to open the hands, with the arms widening the air around them, who will not speak except with the bottom. We study the death of the classic together with idiocy, it is the whole present reality, they are our hairdresser friends, fantastic triumphs of hay. Evil says, they are already evil lady but they wanted to go on television later, before it was just one day of their life instead it is a secret. Follow the arrow but for sure there's an exit at the end, come back I'll bring it to you later, ok. The usual closing is not true but, I'm not wrong, you say everything because you say everything. Check the packaging plus the content is if you also want the quality of what you buy, then at the same time you see who you really were, is if you recover another person like you staying in evil. Even now there are those who will wake up for the death of the classic, it is an image outside of time, fond of the ailments, while on another segment of the sidewalk, you find the classic contemplation of the work. Object and person are an untreated, the world seems uninhabited, cold. Remain silent, speak who is right, don't worry figured, if fears are reality you too have committed a crime punishable by the Italian legislature.

The classic foods are excellent for filling the strangest things, capable of resembling happiness is therefore to other classic things, as we have never spoken before because anyway you see that your reality, the effectiveness, but excuse your general affairs are not going well and, your good? say nothing more, time has passed, memories remain in the memory, who does not know how to speak is a line upstairs that you find it. I wish you a good day, is if it always happens to you without paying for your death. We study how life works, whether it was you or someone else the interest of which he said, of the voice cut the lack, the misery, the deficiency, the decadence as who knows what those people wanted or what we give in object to better understand even today all the other realities, or why someone denounced your or my evil. An eviction, a manifesto, why misery is ruining us, what is wrong with us, or if there are mistakes in the speech as we speak and in our actions. Misery, for me misery is like living all together and having the same wrong thought, about a common thing. They are acts of fascism... you see it's the right word that frees us, the right medicine to our solutions, every word rightly describes the entity of which the speech or the problem is relative, sometimes a calculation of sums create a basis in the total, since you are already in America.

You torture the modern Calabrian mind, have the factories in today's world to create the products that you had to do, what interested you today was not you but come on, where ends your money? who wanted the audio of the municipality to ruin what was already there, to rebuild it together. It has already happened what you want to be now, but the waiting time is too long, but a week is enough to record everything you can do in your life, so we must not be unfounded, we must not do anything to have. See who's talking to you! The lowest of the places, you still want to joke... you don't realize how you want to get to Cosenza. Two points for your business there, but to be bad is to be robbed, uh, in debt. Okay, what do you forget about what's going on in your head, why you can't move? Whose money, whose life? Each of us lives beyond one of the currents here, more and more, you see that dream attached to your window is your real life, you want to say it, you're not that monster.

Being deaf, yes, but what you do not feel is the

life of others, if you are not always careful you do not realize, because the evil you do it yourself out of habit, you do not live on the surface to support a week the wrong things not to follow, the mistakes of a life for what your life means. What the state doesn't exist, one doesn't have what's his. The trivial, the bananas, you have to choose a day to stop thinking about it, find the wrong choice so as not to always lose, you are a good plus your parents, are things that you do not know about the margins, we need to talk about where you go out and the perfect reality, which is about as a payment including cents. A piece of advice is within your person the function, there are unknowns in your identity / person are revealed in the present that you live today, the air, your entity, time, that word of evil where your segment continues or, the ugly expression the law does not speak, what will happen today? Who you live is not, it will be legal problems. What you live, tell me who you are, who wants to overcome you, who wants in the general sense, where will your conception of the real sense of things and people, you don't even imagine how deep your good is in our days, let it go everyone knows maybe it has some short cuts, or maybe they make you pass for good evil. Exploited, mocked and beaten... they don't talk, exploited and mocked so as not to declare that the truth is the only God hanging in heaven, what really reminds you of your identity or even how miserable that evil is.

Fakes, rats, deceivers, who's double-crossing? the light blinds. Truth is true God, good but spirit, still today in heaven closed within a triangle. Our Boy-Glass have nothing to do with the comparison, trust me you're not like that, you'll have the strength of a judge because someone can steal what was in your yesterday, no one will do your past more you'll be the person they're looking for, it will be false as it's true that you've already finished it, you'll overcome it too uh, with your car. It's hard not to believe you, you really don't see what's outside your window, but it's the most basic subject for your modern person, that is, alive, what is certain. You made a mistake then, all things continue and people are there even if you don't know them, and you don't have a relationship with them, what do you want to know about today if there is evil? well, point one as I wanted to tell you just now also wanted you, then yes there is also goes in the oven or in jail, here look out of your room are all gone is what he wants, then keep on turning are not people you know, is tell me who makes you pack an evil, bye. You don't know a good, laugh... you have to be what you are, what you created in the past but, when there's no good anymore, you won't be there, that's it. Tell me who's talking is why you're crying, why it's so hard. Empty people denounce you, we are in a state of arrest while friends told us that since that moment, since then we were free! it has always been a daily question the prison here in our house. Who are all the people? You feel like an evil, a rat, an insect or a devil. In your notebook there is the solution, in all those books you have in the bookstore or, in music CDs, because people from the bottom of their lives write about no to negative or, anti-Christian existence. What you see is the greatest historical epoch or, in the near future that we can have in the end, it can help you that it is always all the people more you, to live now. I hope you will understand, emptiness is not really ideal for living, be careful who speaks to you in our days, we are not at most a human being, we continue to fall, we are our people, so it would be your skin close to the real disease, it is forget that they lose entire nations, there are static forms of existence that are repeated for a certain period or, things that are not said like people. Now from here you're going to a certain number of days, of things.

I salute you, G.

16.
The quality of the Sun

31.03.2010

"Classic there is a world of people who will not under-stand today, the topic is closed. Retro progress... what do you want to do? The rest of reality is difficult, you know, you have to make a speech."

The reality of our objectivity as a whole to exist in a quadriphonic has its beauty, the future is an unknown? who spoke, who knows what he wanted. You've managed to come out of it always need to make a speech, have fun then get so tedious, in our beloved nation. The quality of life, of your resistance, of what you can be, what you are represents your expression. Where have you gone to end up, a piece of advice you always tell everyone everything, that thing they brought you is not working and has already lost. Life is a continuous movement, a revolution, a journey where you are present, where we ended up, which would be two hours after the things you did not do anymore, the objective realities you created. Well, the more things you've been made to do, the more important people you've made. Here you pay for all the bad weather in the world is nothing, maybe it doesn't work for them... think they'll denounce you if it doesn't work, or because you gave them your software then, because yours is going on, that is, they beat you up, you see what a bad difference! one stop, continue afterwards.

If your husband is an evil, your chances are forbidden, your good dies like in a fire in the great Amazonian forest. Now you've just entered into a fantasy or a dream: who would be an evil, bring me back the good, it's the story of your artificial-organic dysfunction or, of your vital sphere when you talk about that, it's our friends who didn't believe me or didn't even know who I was, on the other hand they didn't have a clear idea who they were, remember what I wrote to you is repeated in the future or, it's the future, we feel in the near future, in the meantime look at your face, the earth must be far away from your face. A remote past is a past but, it's your life more than five years ago, then if you stop joking I'll talk more seriously, who is not a biological transsexual is a candy for ceremonies, here you can say everything there no, now find the keys to the human home. It is the story that returns because it was built to stay today, your story that returns calmly I could colour your life.

Your is someone else instead, will be a thief of ideas, of personality I say maybe he will have problems with the law, people are looking for your fake real, not us because these days is contemporary to say all the words to buy your idea, to your neighbour. Be careful to go straight, though, and to the fascists. We are still alive, struck by the Sun and age, falsified, lied and betrayed in quantity is quality... who knows who has to come. Your best friend is your first traitor, are you lost? It will be the air or time whoever you want to talk to us at eight o'clock in the morning on Sunday, everyone will have an imperial Romanity led by some clerical-fascist circles, problems are the parasites of now, towards our Monday that sees Wednesday and Friday. Who knows why you don't talk after all, maybe they want to convince you to psychologically kill Bill Gates. Every little being has all the qualities of life, dearly beloved of my contemporary state, not the air or gas of a concentration camp. Well, bye-bye good day, since you're in Italy.

At the bottom of the glass we fall to the edge of the precipice of existence, an attack persists where humans are not interested. We gain the emptiness and we do not speak because it seems to us a speech already made or, not in accordance with the canons, you are lost? what do you want to find in these sleeping people. Your advice, your complaints have another thought, a custom is our Commune. The silence sometimes ruins because it doesn't recite us or, we miss the book with the instructions of today's time, we are continually offended, beaten up, there is always need. Where do you want to find it is not in the other room or, there by you, it's true we are unique pieces but who knows! Information is important or, your main culture, the serene air of those who have a behaviour of other people alive or dead. Works more than facts, you always have something to do today. You are a living or a perverse world like a still life uh, a plant with few shoots to the branches. Your reality is always there, it finds you where you are at this time, even if you don't know it or you are not me. Look there at that distant ignorant world, so your revolution can begin: who will all these butchers be? Bring the tools of the trade to those in the trade.

" …because who doesn't exist? Who doesn't have his tools there? You know, maybe people think they'll come later. It's my mom's shop next door."

It is a It is a bit complicated to find your person in a big sea when the world, you declare the truth, you have lived in your country, the week is over today. You'd like to do your own publicity but there's too little money, too few dreams, the sign of fascism is on our sky tomorrow, you're still in trouble or, at that famous herringbone in your mouth, if there's a blowfish in your mouth, it was your fault for what's happening today. We're all going to die… find it, even if you have the name, find it, who knows maybe it's there next to you, now go away, here in my house it's not suitable, it doesn't conform. It always seems the same movie as who they say on the radio didn't even understand who or what they're interested in, maybe he wanted to be me on a statue.

I'm in an address on a street for the history of all and posterity, because I have the law and my wallet an evil wants too much, it marks too much, one day we will grow up and maybe we will perish, how serious it was. It was and it is so you do not disappear, if in case you die, the works that are, will have been tomorrow, what is today is forever. You were, you will never be, what you wanted to be ten minutes ago. Please walk, today is the day of cakes, the amiable theme of good appetite. You're still hungry, it's ten o'clock in the morning, you're like the things that satisfy Italians and nationals, Japanese and Germans like nougat on the feast of St. Joseph. Do you feel offended in the back, persistent in the air? From today, not even a leaf moves anymore, so tomorrow goes on, after what happened last week, you sleep in a sleep of vomit, someone says it, uh, look how severe the good was, it also means how useful tomorrow is, now what will you do without your Nobel Prize.

The day has taken another colourful form again, there's crowds in the cafeteria will be almost ten in the morning and our price takes taste, wields form, price that must always be low for an ego that must not be respected. The cut was a heresy that you wear, you will not stay because you are not, or perhaps you are, without your thing. This is called getting out in front of the plane's engine access, that's it. The world and words are as busy as the pledges of your day today.

Good day human being alive today, G.

17.
Do you have any other ideas

28.04.2010

"It was already a little too late when you arrived last week, the heaviest functions come after the first three words. You always fall back at a certain time, but often these days you feel much behind."

Who knows what that bureaucrat wanted, was our neighbour or a thousand people put together, we all have the same problems, we are all equal before the law. Dear insecure gin gin Can that you have yet to arrive, they were not so terrible those, machine gun, a human being goes, continues even with his car when he gets off then everyone already knows or, our complaint and / or friends have "arrested" the habitat, now follow the arrow that is worse than before. It was in May, but even better in full summer. The heat calms us down like every year, while the accounts oppress us if they don't come back to us, let's say the sentence ends here, why has your honour been lost? You haven't lost it, look where it is next to you, big, real, giant, concrete. You are better off in full happiness, you have something to say if you don't object to a little satisfaction, it is a problem of absence, of present constancy, of contemporary replaced by a changing present, take a break life has always been much shorter than our infinite and finished expectations. Someone is behind you don't stop, don't worry it seems, don't worry it seems, but accentuate a little bit the pace you will see is better. Another coffee? I had a good breakfast, now I light a cigarette and continue the day, it is not always so bad habit to say the same things, for what is worth a personal representation applied to a language and society. A reality comes during the day as 'the favourite dream exists in the phone, how many things are not said during the week, so I wish you a good continuation, your segment, your secret, the projection of the Sun towards you.

Italy and the world aren't completely free, you find forgers of themselves and prisoners at liberty, in quantity, you who don't have to know anything so evacuated for the rest of your life, plus they leave us with beautiful jester, in one place. We will grow up, time lingers from the ruins not in distractions, until we reach where the Sun shines the day in its magnanimous light, we will certainly be alone where we ended up tonight, I know the place of perdition to say the least. The soul doesn't even recognize yourself, what happened to you is tell me why nobody speaks to you. In the general sense because you don't talk in the silence of a mean and stingy desert like the money we will earn, with no sense of hour in minute. Would we really have lost? Lost free people, what happened? Where did it happen? Who happened? One at a time of non-word, buried in the house, in and behind a concrete wall as kids when playing. They just wrong the home address was not true that we are all the same as the fascists, ignorance buries us. Here, stay and see how our city's world moves tomorrow morning, without touching anything. Who are they talking about? God or misery, the world is ugly or destitute with gasoline that cheats those who do not live in it, but reality tells you this because in the end you are dead, because your God instead of being dead advises you and is alive, you look what is yours. At the next one, there is for sure, where your school has fired you, because who is a farewell to you that you do not live. Do a little more boys, after seven glasses of wine reality is your meat plus the sky of your room, try to digest better, start counting one, two, three ahead, four then, good evening if the navigator jammed, or our state president did not go to another room to think, now let's go the story continues in the sea of our ideas that someone can understand.

If you do not know our time, the help is useful how long? tell me dear brother who is speaking to you, who organized the day on Monday. Where does the thought sometimes go, in the memory of the year one thousand nine hundred and ninety? Who would I be and the power of the hour that in ten minutes is ready, our obscene advisors that no one must know in the square, what are we still doing here? Say it is too long to say I am lost, memory is a written sheet of paper, where memories are imprinted. Ours are burnt, blossomed. If you stop in ten meters I will let you know that this pile was not there or, it had run out in front of the eyes of good and bad, it takes more freedom than you see. On the other hand, later on you go out, you discover everything, where you are free to walk, you are emancipated to choose humans for your information, I have always taken advantage, I have always taken the freedom to choose people to talk to. You want peace instead, they want war. The Simpsons after the earthquake, I'm worried about what they'll put in jail or chips today. In this world, life is never a game, it's what's in front of you. It was the month of May, but you didn't like the poems at all... so began the sentence of the summer quarrel, who will go wrong this summer, time tests fear or jealousy. To you spring, thawed ice cream that you don't want more words, because the others tell you, you have to get out of the crowd to meet.

Bye, G.

18.
The unknown public

30.05.2010

"Millions of fantasies, thousands of new things, things not or never finished, the objectivity is infinite... that's why the spark of the end of the world has broken out."

What didn't you think someone was talking to you where the dirt ends? how low our home country was. The case is that you do not end, what? what you know, your problems could be everyone's worries as 'the world has changed, you can even go outside the house of other there are only all photocopies of being or errors of form, for example you were five minutes ago, not really a past or you can see the expression of the girls who changed color, but the big buildings do not disappear are the real function of the program that takes us to the next coffee.

The living heart of concreteness, we are watching "sign" his Da Vinci code, I'm also tired of antinoia not monotony, these for God of this century, you have to be more careful how you talk about how to dress. A good coffee is you do not want to do anything, it may be the summer season more things to forget, the force majeure but also hardly need to hurry the mentally organic cleaning of the day.

What to watch today always to stay with your mouth closed, better an accident on the news, everyone knows, who are they all? Tell your fascism, tell him nobody does anything for your person, just shopping. What you often complain about teeth or legs, what you really feel if you see the end of your day, even further down is where you or I went wrong, people in the bar or, the mayor.

You want to leave the bureaucratic part good, good. What is your most dedicated strength, how do you get out of evil if your boyfriend is evil? Moments of boredom, where the world will be in its true home. The seat of the world? Emptiness fills you up. Where you're going wrong now is at lunch, why don't you call it sight. Privacy issues. Who cares about you today.

A beautiful recurrence is the present day, in its great immensity and sunlight, from the morning it heads towards the rest of everything 'l possible. You have wrong people, the rest is not boredom, boredom is death in life. Still to tell you in the present have not done so, you live of a deprived freedom, everyone's solutions in small part participate in yours or, they want to kill you, here you have an answer.

On the sidewalk is always our favourite window, you or what you look at. My tone is gone, the colour is gone but, the consciousness goes on by itself, as the eyes precede the foot to perceive your main colour. In the shop that never changes house number, let alone friends are all false ideas that is your fake goods, there is no such thing as a non-killer way of evil. What do you see today, what do you see who knows what the doctor or, the lawyer two hours ago.

A good is a person who while talking or arguing does not kill any living person in his responsibility, it is continuing with the speech that is, continuing to talk that you discover the truth on the subject, in two hours at all even if you do not know who you're talking to, because you do not know who you are on this day, they have rebuilt us with emptiness is not say the true things because we have them inside empty, talking to someone else you will realize that has Ceres beer, around.

Of us that possibilities are life, we don't have to think about anything anymore, only about the awakening of the world in the false, where humans are false or imaginary in their primary interests, about the false idols of the year zero ten and, the cuts we carry in our faces. Actually, I'll tell you what it's like to be sick, they will be people who want to occupy your chair and your person, look what your neighbour wants to say today, how hard it is to tell him because he also wants to know what happened to him last week without being with you.

A masked evidence, that's what I was saying on that day! Now I am at peace because in this world you become and then, you remain what you are worth. Can't you see that? That's what an evil, a parasite, a thief tells you. Have a nice day, bye, use some Band-Aids, alcohol and cotton.

What help are you missing? It was probably too good. The person is afraid to talk because they think they're not being fair or, to be mocked. It is greater the misery that the horrible includes the entire bust, to talk you can but wait is still early for lunch, I would not leave you like this, even though I'm getting ready to go out. Today is Sunday, a good holiday because you're a living person, look you're alive, it's you, it's the law that tells you it's you. Art is life, objects for art are the most important thing, you are an art object.

Write it because you don't see your flower, reality and truth are like two different people, so comes the night that prepares the day, after don't say anything, it's not a dream anything when you're awake, don't say those bad word.

See you soon, G.

19.
Summer settings

29.06.2010

"A day like any other, the road is travelled, don't forget, not all fantasy is good to continue tomorrow without a... I told you so."

The head must remain connected to the feet always, a hard childhood   trash steals us or, it's us who steal the reality of another, you want me to tell you that people are not in a human, who is in charge here has not yet understood what is the head that operates this indecent "the day", are the realities that have not been changed or worked today, everything goes where the curb of the road has a wall to go bump into us. I know everything is known, everything is already accomplished, as everything happened with the advent of Jesus Christ, everyone knows, I am all ah! ah! What a bloodline wants today, a vial is better. Affirms the truth you cannot escape from hunger, good breakfast we are all again in this place to decide ours today, please.

So, if you also know a lot about material things, the substantial ones don't change, if they don't turn into others different from before, you just have to listen to some good music the one you like. A line of morning fever will wake us up alone, in another distant city, when at night the captains, that is the mayors, keep us away from each other with traditions that are covered with weekly storms. A "I" will no longer exist only the voice, thank you to move that gun or, rifle that shoots as soon as you say a vowel a little more open. The state does the evil to you, it does the evil then, you can fill those empty windows with a spray can of whipped cream. Today the wonder of life could not lose its clear splendour, when it will shine the day of the victory of the real ones, sorry if I live above the habits of everyone every day, like a frieze, a monument or, a status symbol. Everything repeats itself until it's in place forever, from the moment you turn on, me or whoever. One day it is as it is, dear, the compliment is still far away.

The environment with the trees and benches in the pictures, it's all false Mr. Captain in the vein, where you start, people get tired, no one tells the truth, under that malignant form is pagan that supports us. It's wrong what they say because the beam should be superior, maybe your little thought has really passed but, you care, look at it this way, it's you know where you go to find an Italy covered so big that it's difficult to find me. Your limit, write it on a wall, don't speak anymore, speak that... see now there's no one there anymore, what else could matter, it's still your person who doesn't say it, we're almost at the next stop, the decisive one, another day of love where you'll have to be, where you'll be, you know what you'll have to laugh then there are such big problems this morning, fake fascists with a gun who want to kill for freedom. Today's problems, so the Sun has some strange lights and emotions modified by people who don't want your good, so that 'your being instead of all good exists even in evil. Exceptions are people high up in the city... so then, your love will see it, how strange it is, but who knows what it is today in the year zero ten, if you want in July, look at that beautiful sea. Time passes around us and you can't tell who we are, do you need a Band-Aid? Who knows what that plane wanted, what it flew, what it left from, in Italy you never finish, the class of being alive, the class of your Mercedes, who is outside, who is inside, who is working nowadays.

Who knows what it means to be alive today, what will have happened to you or, to me and all of us alive because everything happened the same. Strange, everything is strange after being in the square today, inside what you don't want me to tell you. The end of everything, of the world, of you come on, go on in the kitchen something always happens, you woman decipher people and environments, in your eyes the sea, don't you know me? there are points and there are areas, there is no one.   Wanting, flying... Italy! What you don't understand in your country is also in your city or, of your city is in your city. The rhetoric of what, the thing, the other thing, who told you who is who. What has happened, has been, everything you say now is new, sincerely true or, you and your favourite and infinite desires. What happened on Saturday morning, it may be what you thought happened so it happened then it may happen again in ten minutes... I'll shut up now.

It was a time, an era, a day to live, a dream that will not come to pass as one is already dead for everyone, classified and cloned in quantity, what was freedom? Have you already been modified or have you missed the bus? What represents your life today, is the largest amount, they have already done it all day for you and for everyone, because you do not exist, they do not make you believe you exist or, you do not know me. Do you want to say something about the present? What's going on in the City Hall? Who ruined us? You have another coffee, see you later. They are already free you know, there are people who like to hear about them, your free time becomes your free time, they have discussions under voice for topics of general importance.

It must have happened to you this morning, where the trouble is, I've noticed that it's a time problem, like now what or how to proceed, now or later. Who are people who are sick? Who were you talking about, your parents? Where does your room end, on this day where you are awake, in this year zero ten you have to hide from the people of the state that they are your evil, because you know that you don't go ahead in the offense, they didn't win me those who won, what was supposed to win then there are the fortuitous. You when, where, you have the desire to joke and the weight of your responsibility, of your work, is enormous. Who knows what will happen to everyone today, if you want me to tell you, they will be zombies for the peace of all or, the serenity of our spider god, it would also be the deepest part of no. You're talking to me, I'm crying. Aren't you the person? Please, in the other room as in a dream you are alive, because everything has already happened to you, because we are already alive, that's where the State helps us, if we are already alive.

Go on towards your goal to finish this, things happen where they are in their being, their property gives, we still have to dear Italian or extra, from a to z and from z to a, everything else is boring or empty of us. What ignores your truth, what does someone who is at home today want to make? Have we moved on? The boys get confused between the game and serious things then, they get lost. Emptiness and then what you had to say, what you had to do. You don't feel like a thief.

The past, even an hour ago, is not erased, the problem is a shoebox in front of you. How unclear is mine, yours, theirs, conscience and knowledge, what others have said well is what really happened.

Have a good trip, G.

20.
Physics of light radiation

15.07.2010

There has always been a network to lean on, how come we will not go back to where we were, perhaps this would create many problems depending on the age we are attributed today? In the world there are always the same people, the fact is always the same as a house, a building to say, what happened to someone twenty years ago, it could happen even now. The same person has always come to say no to an idea, for goodness sake no, a positive is not always the same. It's as if memory is a toy when you don't play with anything here, then the end of a game is the beginning of truth, of objectivity or simply when you get back on the road to go home. Here it's almost seven o'clock, it's almost dinner time, it's not a bad thing I say to myself, after a day's work. In the last few days I've been thinking about what was the main function of our society that I've known for a long time, was its identity, since it's exhausted or we would need to be declared its completeness, but since we live there it wouldn't be necessary... here then we would need a new party or a program, a software... if it's necessary to tell you that realities are repeating themselves, so in a few periods the same thing will happen. All in all it seemed to me subjective an extra, you are already later than before, how to find peace in those actions that are best known over time to find themselves especially at home, even leaving aside social and moral ideals, thinking about the objects appearing not as they should be but so that what is not desired does not exist, as if we will not see a better day or, to think that a mistake is the cause, the effect of a day. Generally speaking, we have to keep ourselves in this world that is imprecise, it is the same thing to say that we have to imagine it in order not to dream it, the only way to imagine reality is to dream the same dream that then becomes mathematical and concrete. Real is a dream that is imagined to be made real, the structure of a magic to live a life that pays the debt that had not been able to pay off or because walls are not knocked down. Tiredness and freedom do the rest, even of people who are missing everywhere but who exist somewhere else, in a city or provincial space, more than ever in a municipality, as what will make me believe that today is the mirror of yesterday and tomorrow only a daily, money and darkness, immense expanses of time to the pulping without respite, without stopping until the end, until the very end, until the very end where I have always thought.

This world is in danger, no, it never was, it can only be that an end is a beginning, holes are not part of ideal spheres, life is a game not madness, what has been can only be or, seemingly, an opening to an illusory world. The right is not only in front of you but a total of what you see or hear, crying over misfortunes only makes them yours, we must eliminate all problems being careful not to eliminate ourselves, what does it matter what exists outside or around us, another cigarette could be enough to find a complete peace in the end you find it even only in yourself, because when you are with one, you are with a hundred. Isn't that normal? But what does it matter, after all, everything is normal since we are standing up and we can do it. What can you do? How many things we could do, so many and unexpected things, is it bad at a certain age to have unexpected things? Here the law makes it clear that everything is unexpected, as if everything was law. If you look at the world, it's a mistake on which a perfect mathematics is based, in reality a multinational mafia association, criminality in the sense of absence from the planet, a peace that arrives by de facto causes without an act but by absolute positions taken... they abuse and it's normal, the law is silence. In the furrows dug by time it's a bad business not to endure something, yeah but still nobody endures an evil, it's enough to get hurt to be evil. So what they do to produce us an evil to make us look more like is to make the problem disappear at the same time but we have only one solution/access code, the only one they have given us, only one, all the others are incompatible. That light appears, the end of the world, the resistance, did I miss something? I've never lost anything, except money sometimes. I look at the past, past experiences and think what is best for me and my friends. Overcomes everything, overcomes the staff were mostly issues of privacy ... and you find yourself point and start again, however if you overcome go ahead! Stop, no more problems, which are solved in the competence. Look, how many beautiful, sunny days await us. *Bye, G.*

21.

We're already us in ten minutes

31.07.2010

"A trauma was just thinking alive today... I think of you no longer being alive today, what alive means is what decadence is."

Life never stops, the images, we are a decadent, different from alive or white, a socially and stately unassisted, are still the problems never passed, we will be alive with a consciousness of ten years ago. Today the Sun is better than buying a light bulb and through Enel turn it on, who has already won is only God.

You want to set your bones to listen, where you speak are already ten thousand years that I live out of evil, here for ten minutes already, we have not introduced ourselves are your star, the memory that has been lost, the recovery not to understand, not to understand. I know there is still an evil but, what do you prefer for lunch, tell me your public duty, your decadent, is tell me what you lived yesterday, last week, it is much more important what your city of Good says, today is a bit 'confused? free to die, the fashion decays? horrible are the realities that surround us after nine o'clock in the morning, who knows who we will be, we just have to leave do not understand, do not listen, do not believe in others is not a simple thing but, a training, how to play an instrument.

Today all the solutions are on a table, one day the world will heal itself, you'll see all that annoying saying will be eliminated. The law is not the same for everyone, it is called the absence of state for all people and the state itself, as you want we have already won, we are already alone. Open a book by a great artist, listen to a discography, find your descendants see your V-crack.

The end of the discourse happens with his term, the thought stops only with his death. In a river an evil does not stop, so it is a matter of stopping the thought to start the new life. Who knows what else you want to do, just build everything you want to do, other people will be mistreated or, it doesn't work for us. I'm already my life is over, I'm writing to you because your life is over, how do you continue the day? who tells you, who are the ignorant people of Crete, the incompetent. Everything has been resolved up to a certain point since this morning and we are not even there, to understand it is not to be death liners for today. Too many better things, too many things is enough then, there are never too many things, where you look for your mistake today, I should find mine. Only the lowest is said, no one and yet something has been learned who knows, what comes back as the electricity bill uh, hunger.

Or you, who your main eyes don't even know to talk to, we're all completely offended. Is she wrong girl or you great man, theirs have already done it for years, even many, as we want all 'l program for today's resolution to build, it seems a baroque as 'l our ego of now. The world to resist is false, falsified, peace is not yours but others', where are they all? Later they will later, later, later, later, they will be your titles. Today thus comes to an end, as the end of sin our bad day, so it is called dearly lost. Is tomorrow roaring like this the day tomorrow? The favourite crowd, so do the others speak. Beyond your idiot, beyond your manual, down where they want to copy you, in the perfumery of a great classic, one must already know that the unknown is the void beyond the Earth. At the border of life near the earthly death of a young age, what was the end of the world, what will have been in the year two thousand. You wanted a kiss, that's it. The others are so talk, happy birthday love, the evening burns and the morning refreshes us, to say briefly again in this place with the fear that an interest dies, a friend or the end of ourselves, the end of this is what the poor irreverent do not speak, it was not happening to you or, to our audiences but, to those in via x in the same city, the same problem.

The union of the municipality from alderman to citizen, as 'the mayor all. Burials, who wants to take a break? That's you when you were young, your youthful experiences, seen that past mistakes are better to turn off the present. We all live in the same region, nation, country while they have already done a good or, the fast route of a tram. They have already done everything at this hour at dusk in the evening, all 'good! for example if you talk you only hear voices coming from outside with all the problems solved, is you poor mortal who will work from Monday morning, make your peace as a kiwi karate. Who are the zombies, stop, I mean stop, they are what came. The words are finished, just fine, reincarnate the "Carmina: little girls poems". Are also finished the money unfortunately Monday we work, too many rumours after all it was just evening, the one that will come or, the one where we are is not telling you anything else now, so as a joke not to move on to other dances we go on. Only a lament of centuries is said, for me it was last week, irritates that strange burner near the face after all.

In a country or an immense city, we are submerged in the peace of the ecstasy of nowhere, where the power of a lantern will be gone, there were goods beyond this swamp that dirty the body, much bigger than them, in their cars, with their gasoline, only they are many who have already finished living, waiting to be completed. It was just an environment between them, and they don't believe it. Disillusioned... you don't like the word, numb to seem what you are not in the soul. Big business who knows when and how much, marketing business or other theories of how we go on about who we are.

An interest of others is everything, they want to be fake or left where the wind is blowing, no others do not stay in the good, yes they do, only those who speak today is but you could change a lot, how strange is the world, as they say now offended. It is necessary to have only a little calm, it must be calculated in reality, a change, a change may seem an offence. Adagio how heavy is a Marlboro in how many questions of what we have is not we have, the others, the houses, the Sun and the sea. Are we broken down? No one's answering, have the others already left? Are there people who want to build us? The rest of us live abandoned in the absence of a concrete participation, Il Resto del Carlino doesn't write about… it's down, down talking will be what we see the reality of all or a large part of the people then, we are not so many humans, it's in the end just us on an identity card, and we don't do all those goals as many things are not said. In its impossibility, good day. Let's calm down must still be counted for this does not work, then the twentieth century and the inventions, the phone, the stack. The day hurts inside then, go further down the street you can't breathe here, it's okay then there will be melon and ice cream.

Easter was a better day, as was Doomsday. The boys were joking about life, they didn't realize the somatic trouble they'd gotten into. It was now and there was no one there, all those who do not speak in our darkness of the year zero ten will come. What more did you want to do at work Mr Wollas, you have the solutions, tell me why today is going to start well, all well, gorgeous please. Peace doesn't exist because you're alive, it's not bad, de profundis mente is a surgical operation of what you have to do, how many things you don't say, he knew it, he knows it but the work continues.

A state in your absence is not your fault, that doesn't concern you, you're just you, the one in the photo is not the state that isn't at home with the increases, have a good day at least. It was the day of judgment, go take a walk. The judgment wants to take us away, a checkmate to our evils, false Italians, the preferred punctures, the stops of a lifetime, what you want to understand of the rest of planet Earth today, boys and old people. The stops at cards like those on the road, it's just a matter of crying or laughing even for how easy it is to be enemies with yours, it's already here in front of the computer all the good that had to come.

In the absence is where you want or where you don't want, that is, tell me who is speaking now. Today has never existed says but, it is a mistake you have to talk to a good then, even with your body, does not want to understand it are other people: us and our people. The general entity is already established at least until noon, you just wanted the end of that speech until the next time we met. Good or bad, good or bad, good mid-

August, those who have seen each other have seen each other, they met then, they said goodbye.

We have already been the images in the mirror or the people talking, the findings are revelations.

Bye, G.

"So I conclude my third diary, I think it could be interesting and useful for those who want to explore my solutions of this world, in a memory about a not far past that could be the background of today's everyday life. I wish you the best for all the surprises that life has in store for you.
Good luck!"

Gerardo D'Orrico
https://www.beneinst.it

Index of contents

Index of contents

IT'S ALREADY US IN TEN MINUTES

by Gerardo D'Orrico

English translation

by Fatima Immacolata Pretta

Publishing house

TEKTIME

ISBN 9788835411147